On Community and Environment

THE RSA

The Royal Society for the encouragement of Arts, Manufactures and Commerce (RSA) was founded in 1754 with a mission to 'embolden enterprise, to enlarge science, to refine art, to improve our manufactures and to extend our commerce'. Believing that a thriving economy was the determining factor in the development of a civilized society, the RSA's founding Fellows sought to encourage innovation, the acquisition of new skills and the creation of new markets.

The RSA today uses its independence and the resources of its international Fellowship to stimulate debate, develop ideas and encourage action in its main fields of interest: business and industry, design and technology, education, the arts and the environment. The RSA Fellowship (now numbering nearly 21,500 in the UK and abroad) is drawn from almost every vocation and provides a resource of expertise and practical experience on which the Society can call.

The RSA is good at forming partnerships, at working with others to increase the pressure for change. The Society provides a forum for discussion within which ideas may be shaped and action stimulated. Often the process starts with a lecture, seminar or conference, then may follow active promotion through a project, campaign or award scheme.

Current projects include Redefining Schooling, PROJECT 2001, Focus on Food, Forum for Ethics in the Workplace, the RSA Student Design Awards, and The Arts Matter programme (see also the back pages of this book).

For more information please write to The Director, RSA, 8 John Adam Street, London WC2N 6EZ or telephone 0171 930 5115. (Fax 0171 839 5805, Website http://www.rsa.org.uk)

RSA

ON COMMUNITY AND ENVIRONMENT

*A selection of lectures organized by the
Royal Society for the encouragement of
Arts, Manufactures and Commerce*

Gower

Published by
Gower Publishing Limited
Gower House
Croft Road
Aldershot
Hampshire GU11 3HR
England

Gower
Old Post Road
Brookfield
Vermont 05036
USA

The authors of these lectures have asserted their rights under the Copyright, Designs and Patents Act 1988 to be identified as the authors of this work.

British Library Cataloguing in Publication Data
On community and environment: a selection of lectures organized by the
Royal Society for the Encouragement of Arts, Manufactures and Commerce
1. Environmentalism 2. Environmental policy
3. Environmentalism – Social aspects
I. Royal Society of Arts
333.7

ISBN 0-566-08106-7

Lecture sponsors: Severn Trent Plc, Save the Children Fund, Whitbread PLC, KPMG, Peter Scott.

Text designed by David Brown and Bob Vickers and printed in Great Britain by The University Press, Cambridge.

CONTENTS

FOREWORD

This is an inspiring book because it shows that ordinary people can collectively work to change their own local environments for the better. And that is important, because it is all too easy to fall into the mindset that it takes the kind of event which happens only once every five or seven years (Rio Earth Summit 1992, Kyoto Climate Summit 1997) and involves the cooperation of every environmental minister of every government in the world plus about 30,000 hangers-on. It doesn't and needn't, and there are dozens of stories here to prove it and to show how.

The book also shows how people can work outwards from their own bailiwicks to intervene against powerful forces in other places, sometimes remote ones on the other side of the world. But, as Derek Osborn reminds us here, we do also need Kyotos. And he shows that there, as elsewhere, there's a problem he calls tractability: certain kinds of environmental problem (the ozone layer) can be solved because the conditions are right, while others (climate change, biodiversity) are just very difficult: we don't even understand enough about the basic problem, let alone practicable answers.

Jonathon Porritt, in contrast, pronounces himself an incurable optimist. He thinks that the scientists are gaining control, that the green movement is breeding a generation of techno-fixers, and that new agencies are flexing their muscles. And Guy Thompson, one of the responding lecturers, has much the same message. Yet his colleague Julie Hirigoyen is sceptical: she points to the American reluctance at Kyoto to accept fuel reduction targets. How do you choose between these views?

Almost certainly by accepting that some problems are inherently difficult and need more work, and by agreeing that the environmental debate has to be carried through in every community in every country. It won't be easy to persuade a Texan, who may drive 300 miles to shop, that this no longer represents a sustainable way of life; after all, the nearest decent bunch of shops may be that far away. But views do change, and radically: look at the way we British have accepted successive fuel duty hikes. And look at the evidence, from Amory Lovins' lecture, that environmentally-designed buildings can save money and make you feel good, all at the same time.

As Lovins and Ernst von Weizsacker have pointed out in their influential Factor Four theory, we've got our economics upside down, and need to turn it the right way up: instead of economizing on people and putting them on the unemployment scrapheap, we need to economize on resources. So read this collection – and then, if inspired, go out and find out more.

Professor Sir Peter Hall, FBA

Head of Planning, Bartlett School of Architecture

INTRODUCTION

This book contains a selection of RSA lectures whose common thread is the importance of community and our relationship to it. As the world shrinks and communications, travel and distance take on new meaning, the earth's environmental problems will seem more visible and the communities in which we live and work ever more important to conserve.

This group of lectures is particularly relevant to the RSA, which throughout its existence has been working on sustainability and good environmental practice projects. One of its biggest achievements has been the planting of over 60 million trees in an awards scheme from 1758 to 1821 and many of today's woods are the direct result. In recent years the RSA has produced award schemes such as the Pollution Abatement Technology Awards and the RSA Environmental Management Awards to raise the awareness of key environmental issues and to stimulate the development of good practice. For further information on the RSA's current programme of activity see the back of the book.

The book opens with eight lectures, from the Handing on the Baton series, by distinguished British environmentalists: Susan Clifford, co-founder of Common Ground; Derek Osborn, Chairman of UNED/UK and Jonathon Porritt, Director of the Forum for the Future, with texts in between by up and coming younger environmentalists, each responding to the former's comments and 'taking up the baton' for the next generation.

Susan Clifford calls her lecture 'reweaving the local' and she describes the work of the campaigning charity, Common Ground. Apple Day and the Parish Maps Project are ingenious ways to reconnect people to their local place and Common Ground has successfully put local distinctiveness onto the environmental agenda. It champions the importance of common culture, everyday nature, ordinary history, familiar places and local involvement. Emma Must, the Twyford Down campaigner and Mark Redman, an agricultural scientist, respond by drawing on their own experiences. Mark Redman focuses on the phrase 'positive parochialism' as embracing the local dimension.

Following on this theme, Derek Osborn focuses on international activity and how it might be possible to make a sense of common purpose for everyone. He stresses that environmental problems and issues do not stop at national boundaries and he draws on the legacy of the 1992 Earth Summit in Rio and the vital development of Local Agenda 21. He is currently involved in planning for the 2002 Earth Summit which will be the next big opportunity to push forward the sustainable development agenda and will give the next generation a chance to set the agenda for future environmental action. Hugh Raven adds to this by saying that there is an important role for not only governments, but also for business in resolving the incompatibility between international trade and international environmental laws.

The series concludes with Jonathon Porritt optimistically predicting that with fast-developing global communications, information technology, policy and community spirit, the world's environmental problems will diminish. He argues that environmentalists, traditionally pessimistic people, have reasons to be cheerful and should be optimistic as it is optimism that produces more action. Pessimism just disempowers people.

The two former Forum for the Future scholars, Julie Hirigoyen and Guy Thompson, responding to Jonathon Porritt, are also fairly optimistic. Julie Hirigoyen also tackles the problem of over consumption in the West; Guy Thompson says that the environment is no longer the sole preserve of biologists and conservationists, as it was ten years ago. We are all becoming environmentalists and the importance of local action is stressed by both of them.

On the international level Professor Vitit Muntarbhorn from Chulalongkorn University in Bangkok in his RSA/Save the Children Millennium Lecture, uses the UN Convention on the Rights of the Child to highlight the need to respect the views of children in helping us build a just society. He believes that children can do much to improve their own lives and exert influence for good in their communities and in the wider world. Children's participation as active citizens, even if they do not have legal citizenship, is vital.

The following two lectures by John Edmonds and Andrew Mawson are also linked by the theme of community involvement. John Edmonds draws on William Morris and says that it is human nature for people to enjoy undertaking worthwhile work and pay often gets in the way of any discussions about it. The contradiction is that we so often only view paid work as 'work'. Some of John Edmonds' concepts are brought to life in Andrew Mawson's lecture on the Bromley by Bow Centre. In this deprived part of East London, the Centre has been set up to explore and exploit the entrepreneurial potential of the local people.

Next the built environment is discussed. Michael Holyer, the Chairman of Habinteg Housing Association, and Richard Best, Director, Joseph Rowntree Foundation, focus on housing and the needs for the next millennium. Michael Holyer describes the work of Habinteg Housing Association by telling the story of twins, Jack and Jill, one able-bodied and the other disabled, and the concept of homes for life. By investing now in homes that are flexible and adapt to our changing needs throughout our lives, we will reduce costs and upheaval for the future. The lecture is complemented by Richard Best's discussion of the need for the much publicized 4.4 million extra homes by 2016. 'Smart Homes' are a way forward and the technology, such as remote controls to operate curtains, open windows and lock doors, is already with us. There needs to be a holistic approach to the housing problem. The Joseph Rowntree Foundation is leading the way, helped by housing groups such as Habinteg. Richard Best concludes by saying that the aim is to build stronger communities where we can live more harmoniously together.

Amory Lovins, the well-known American architect and environmentalist, discusses in his lecture the different elements that go into designing a truly 'green' building. He includes examples from Chicago, Leicester, Amsterdam, California and the White House and explains that green architecture goes beyond the immediate environmental impact, but aims to heal the community, and regenerate and restore the environment.

Paul Ekins, the environmental economist, begins his lecture by defining sustainable development. He has devised a list of conditions that would have to be satisfied before a development process could be called 'sustainable' and then goes on to discuss the contribution of architecture to this process, which, as he reminds us, does not only mean new buildings, but also upgrades of old buildings. Architects have a duty to make buildings more energy efficient and also more pleasing and harmonizing for the communities which use them, but, realistically, he also brings affordability and government action into the argument.

Finally, the architect Alexandros Tombazis poses the question 'should green architecture be something different?' His lecture brings practical experience from working as an architect in Athens about sustainable architecture and focuses on aesthetic, sensory and holistic issues, as well as the design process itself.

This book covers a wide range of subjects and views brought together from all over the world. The lectures are printed here in specially edited versions. The RSA would like to thank the lecturers and sponsors who supported the RSA 1997/98 lecture programme on which the publication is based.

STRAIGHT LINES
AND GREAT CIRCLES:
REWEAVING THE LOCAL

SUSAN CLIFFORD

Joint Coordinator and Founder Director, Common Ground

It is quicker, when travelling far, to take the line of a great circle. You can move at great speed; in little more than a day, you can be on the other side of the world. You have stepped beyond the realities known to every other century in the earth's history. You are learning faster, taking greater leaps of theoretical and practical knowledge than ever before. You are controlling the environment in which you live and move. Beside you on this waning planet someone begs in a doorway, someone walks miles every single day to fetch water and wood, someone has been taught how to supply beans for distant supermarkets and has forgotten how to grow their own food. Increasingly places look and feel the same, cultures and geographies are being ironed out by global giants.

A sense of the local and the possible
Turning to face the inequities, the homogenization, the waste — how can one person change things? The breakthrough comes with the recognition that you do not have to face up to the whole complexity alone. Common Ground has taken on a corner of complexity and endeavoured to infect others with a sense of the possible. Convinced of the importance of the local, we try to

inspire and inform, encourage and empower people to stand up
for their everyday environment, their links with common nature
and ordinary histories – the complexity and richness which make
a place, with its significances, meaning and identity.

Leaving professionals to argue for and look after beleaguered
species, resources or places in the name of caring for the
environment seemed to Common Ground to be exclusive,
reductive, unecological and doomed to failure. For us the
challenge has been to argue for the ordinary, the everywhere, the
everyone. We have had to look beyond facts and figures to what
makes people care. We are chronically aware of the need to give
values a platform, to help people express and argue for those
aspects of their attachments and understandings of living in the
world which are not conducive to quantitative evaluation.
Humanity and imagination are important in helping us to create
more sustainable and more convivial patterns of life. Fundamental
to our philosophy is an understanding that all people can and
should be involved in creativity and decision-making about their
place.

Common Ground projects

THE PARISH MAPS PROJECT
The Parish Maps project encourages people to come together to
exchange what they know of their place, to search for more
knowledge, to discuss what they value as much as what others have
told them is important. Charting what is valued becomes a
stepping stone to working out ideas for involvement and change
guided from within. The process is about learning by doing. No
formula is laid down. Common Ground has offered a philosophy
and produced materials to help. It encourages contact with other
Parish Mappers to share examples and ideas. At its best this social
endeavour brings people to exploration of overlapping interests,
lifts courage and begins to spill over into the making of agendas
and practical action.

SAVE OUR ORCHARDS

Out of a programme called Trees, Woods and the Green Man came the Save Our Orchards campaign in 1988. It was driven by the realization of how many traditional orchards we were losing; 90 per cent of Devon's orchards had disappeared since 1965. The campaign has included alerting individuals and groups, local authorities and government agencies to the drastic loss of orchards and the wealth they contain. In 1990 we initiated Apple Day on 21 October as a way of giving people an opportunity to celebrate the wide variety of the fruit we can grow (over 6,000 varieties of eating and cooking apples alone). We have had considerable success: old orchards are now eligible for grant-aid from the Ministry of Agriculture, Fishery & Food's Countryside Stewardship scheme and local authorities, groups and communities across the country are saving old orchards, planting new ones and beginning to create community and school orchards.

ORCHARDS IN THE CULTURAL LANDSCAPE

In addition to their seasonal beauty, orchards offer a wonderful example of local distinctiveness, biodiversity and the cultural landscape. Hard work over generations has produced fruit varieties and orchard types that are particularly suited to their places, that have produced regional and local recipes, customs and songs. Traditional orchards are also rich places for wildlife.

In 1992 we began promoting the idea of community orchards for cities, schools and hospitals. This work will be extended with funding from, among others, the Department of the Environment, Transport and the Regions. Imagine a place run by and for local people, a place for festive gatherings, communal food growing, contemplation, play, cider and juice making, animal grazing, sharing skills of tree planting, pruning and grafting, nurturing biodiversity, building a new mutuality between nature and culture. This project has tremendous power to involve new people and spark off novel ideas and practice, above all to build people's confidence and knowledge to do things for themselves on their own doorstep in the city as well as the country.

TREE DRESSING DAY

A second innovation emerged from this work. Tree Dressing Day is about encouraging people to draw on the worldwide traditions which focus significance on trees. The aspiration has been to help people build responsibility towards mature trees by creating a cross-cultural festival on the first weekend in December for trees in the public domain. People have come together to explore the potential of lighting trees and hanging things on them, creating dance, poetry and drama around them. Working with the whole range of the arts has helped those involved in the environment to reach diverse groups within the community.

Interweaving the arts

With our winnings from the Prudential Award for the Visual Arts (1989) we sought a sculptor to work around their home place intensifying the richness of local distinctiveness and for a photographer to interweave his art with the sculptor's work. Peter Randall-Page had already worked on our model project, New Milestones, exploring what places mean to people who live and work in them and how to express some of that meaning through sculpture.

Peter agreed to work around Drewsteignton, north of Dartmoor, over five years, creating works which respond to the local history and extend the particularity of the place. This would necessitate a continuous dialogue with local people about their knowledge and perceptions and where works might go. Meanwhile and in parallel, Common Ground gave a grant to photographer Chris Chapman to seek out the particularity in the place, to watch the progress of boulder from moor through sculpture yard and back into the landscape.

It is possible to intervene in a place and add to its richness. It is possible to help people to see and feel things they might never have confronted. Common Ground's work wanders through the realms of building, archaeology, history, ecology, landscape, planning, horticulture, farming, cooking, as well as poetry, painting, drama, dance, to inspire people with the richness of involvement in all of the dimensions of everyday places. Peter's work is part of this, in the same way as that of the farmer who has kept Devon Reds for 50 years or the woman creating new uses for local orchard fruit.

Celebrating the commonplace
In coining the term 'local distinctiveness' we have tried to break free from compartmentalization and preoccupation with the beautiful, the rare and the stately to help people explore, express and savour what makes the commonplace particular. Places are not just physical surroundings. They are a web of rich, evolving understandings between people and nature, peoples and their histories, people and their neighbours, in cities, suburbs and the countryside. Most people understand places and value them because they mean something to them. Small things may breathe significance into the streets or fields. Try to define these things from the outside or on a grand scale and the point is lost.

Local distinctiveness is also about accommodation and change, accumulations and assemblages, not about stratification and preservation. A local culture which has sufficient self-knowledge, identity and self-esteem is confident in welcoming new people and new ideas. Much development and farming activity has been reducing variegation, producing uniformity in housing, high streets, factories, fields which could be anywhere and removing the subtle things which help people hold their knowledge together. Some change removes everything that has gone before.

Local distinctiveness is proving a useful idea at many levels and in many places: evidence is glimpsed in, for example, its influence on policy formulation and practice in landscape work and building conservation in Derbyshire, Hampshire, Warwickshire and Surrey, cultural policy in Kirklees, highways in Devon, community involvement in Herefordshire and the Isle of Wight.

Inspiration from names
Lately we have been working on fields and their importance in culture. Simply using field names as a starting-point is exciting people

to look more closely at what they thought they knew. Ouler Field, Alderlands, Aldermead, Eller Flatt, Aller Bed, the Orles, Woollery Croft, Howler Close – these are all field names implying that alders grow or grew there. Sometimes it is transparent from the name, sometimes a surprise to learn what the medievalists or archaeologists suggest when they are asked to translate the names into current English. Recognizing that most field names are descriptive is interesting but can the names also be used for prescription? Can the conditions be re-established to grow alders there again?

Common Ground has encouraged people into questing for the names of fields local to them, linking farmers, archivists, local historians, amenity groups, wildlife enthusiasts, local councils, as well as environmental organizations. The intention is to bring the names back into common use. Finding names etched into stiles, gates and gate-posts will give walkers a small cue to ponder upon, and knowing names gives one more starting-point for the circulation of local knowledge. The poetry of the names has not escaped us; indeed, in the recent poetry competition on fields which we have run with Blue Nose Poets, names have proved one starting-point for writers.

Our approach is towards positive involvement based on increasing local knowledge and is different from the heavy-handed national pronouncements on the intention to release Green Belt land for a forecast of 4.4 million households in the next 20 years.

The long way round
What next? Common Ground is now turning attention to local distinctiveness and rivers, to our profligacy with water and our willingness to let culverts swallow streams. Pioneering projects include 'Confluence', working with a composer and local people, not only helping them explore and express through music a love of a river (the Stour, which flows through Somerset, Wiltshire and Dorset), but also attempting to change the ways in which we use and abuse water.

It is our belief that what is now called sustainability can work only if we create a culture of wanting to care. Many people who care are put off by the cult of the special, by pedantic practices, powerful interests and the sheer weight of the problems. Yet there are different ways of helping people take some first steps. We have tried to help people to recognize and celebrate what their place means to them as a way of engaging in its future as well as understanding its past and expressing its present. The constant remaking of the local is a multiple endeavour. We believe it will be quicker in the long run to go the long way round, within the greater pattern, to take time and weave it into place.

Note
Information on publications and projects is available from: Common Ground, P.O. Box 25309, London NW5 1ZA.

PRIDE OF PLACE

EMMA MUST

Former Campaigner, Transport 2000 and World Development Movement;
International Programme Manager, ASH

Until 1992, Twyford Down in Hampshire was a great arc of chalk over a mile long. Its rocks had been folded and then eroded across history for 100 million years. People came on the scene later, but even they had shaped its surface for at least 4,000 years, leaving behind them evidence of an Iron Age settlement and a Bronze Age burial site. Latterly – for the last millennium and a half or so, through Roman and Saxon times up to 1992 – the Down had provided a stable and solid backcloth to the evolving city of Winchester. For me, growing up a few miles away, that arc of chalk was etched on the backcloth of my mind.

For 20 long years local people had, through the public inquiry system and the courts, opposed the construction of the missing link of the M3 motorway. But in 1992 the shady avenues of bureaucracy had been exhausted and the bulldozers moved on to Twyford Down. The resulting white scar flashed its warning at the sky, and at the few men who at the tail end of the twentieth century dared to try and dismantle the past. I watched whilst bulldozers gouged out bucket load after bucket load of chalk from the hill and dumped it into the River Itchen at its foot. The swans that were swimming there scattered in terror. That image too is now etched on my mind: white chalk crashing down, white river water splashing up and the white swans fleeing.

Transport policy

Only five years ago this is what British transport policy meant – and it wasn't only a question of one road through one hill, but potentially a thousand roads through a thousand hills by the early years of the twenty-first century. The 1989 roads programme, described by the minister who launched it as the 'biggest since the Romans', meant that everybody everywhere seemed to have a road coming somewhere near them that would destroy forever a beloved landscape or a local community, and bring more and more traffic, noise and pollution into the bargain.

And people simply wouldn't put up with it. That urgent white warning that Twyford Down had flashed at the sky – flashed at the workmen from the Department of Transport – had indeed meant something.

The people's protest

The protest against indiscriminate road-building over the past five or so years has involved everything from people lying in front of massive machines or locking themselves onto bulldozers to driving cars in formation into the fields of a valley, like the proud people of the Calder Valley in West Yorkshire who showed just how it would look with the M1 to M62 link cutting a swathe across it. The protest has involved thousands of people from the Gwent Levels in South Wales, who returned the 'public consultation questionnaire' for the M4 Relief Road complete with the addition of a 'no road' box, carefully ticked. It involved an astonishing spectrum of people from the self-confessed band of 'middle-aged middle Englanders' from Morcombelake in Dorset through to the tree-top tribe at the M65; everyone from travellers with beaded hair to the pleated-skirted Tory ladies of the Home Counties – learning from each other and forming broad alliances.

And the protest has worked. This broad spectrum of people, with its broad spectrum of methods of protest, resulted in a combination of noisy defeats (including Twyford Down, M11,

Newbury) and quiet victories (including Norwich, Woodstock, West Wellow). The roads programme began to crumble.

Reduction in road-building
With the protesters backed up by experts such as the Royal Commission on Environmental Pollution and the Department of Transport's own advisers (who in 1994 concluded what ordinary people have always known: that new roads usually generate more traffic), the roads programme didn't stand a chance. There are now fewer than 37 road-building schemes; in 1989 there were 550. Alternative transport schemes are being seriously considered and there are soon likely to be no more than a large handful of road schemes left in the national programme.

As former Tory Roads Minister, Steven Norris, said in a BBC *Panorama* programme in 1997, 'It's been, in a sense, a gentle but complete U-turn. The great tanker of transport policy is now heading south, where it was previously heading north … it's probably as profound a change as has happened in any Department of State in any sphere of Government over the last 30 or 40 years … the protesters had a message which was fundamentally the right message …'

Part of that message was that people will not easily sacrifice place or community, in this case simply to make way for spiralling traffic growth. Place is precious. There is now layer upon layer of work being carried out by campaigners at local and national level, by progressive local authorities and by government to flesh out the transport alternatives, be it Green Commuter Plans or Safe Routes to School.

The effects of multinationals
On the issue of multinational companies, the World Development Movement (WDM) campaigns to change the policies of governments and businesses in richer countries which cause poverty in the developing world. The combined income of the top

eight multinationals is greater than that of half the world's population; 25 years ago there were 7,000 multinationals and today there are 40,000, controlling over 70 per cent of world trade. Meanwhile, the gap between the richest 20 per cent of the world's population and the poorest 20 per cent has more than doubled in the last 30 years.

The meaning of place

Looking more closely at the effects of multinational corporations on the world's population, I find that one of the biggest categories of problem has to do – once again – with their disregarding the importance of place to people.

One example of this is the situation of the Amungme tribe in West Papua. They are demanding an end to the destruction of their lands, which have been taken over by Indonesia's biggest and most controversial mine, the Grasberg copper and gold mine. This is now being expanded with the backing of a British mining company, Rio Tinto. The mine has ravaged the Amungme's sacred mountain, home to the spirits of their ancestors, silting up their rivers and causing sago crops (the staple diet) to die, as well as destroying their fishing grounds. As an Amungme tribal leader said: 'Freeport [the company which operates the mine] is digging out our mother's brain – that is why we are resisting.'

Permission has now been granted to expand the extent of the exploration by 300 times – to an area larger than Wales. In solidarity with the Amungme's sustained protest against the mine, WDM took the campaign to Rio Tinto Zinc (RTZ) in its home country, demanding that it puts people before profits, and indeed place before profits.

The influence of stakeholders

How did WDM do this? By recognizing that we in the north, as consumers and shareholders, are very powerful stakeholders in multinational companies. We are especially powerful as policy holders of insurance companies and pension trusts – the institutional shareholders of the multinational corporations. Institutions now control 80 per cent of the shares quoted on the Stock Exchange and therefore have the power to turn rhetoric into reality. By putting forward resolutions at AGMs or calling for extraordinary general meetings, institutional shareholders can press for multinationals to seriously consider their impact on the lands and lives of people in the Third World. As an anonymous company chairman was quoted as saying in the *Financial Times* in 1996: 'Sticks and stones may break my bones, but institutional shareholders can fire me. Give me 10 nutters throwing eggs at me any time rather than even one institution casting its votes against re-electing one of my directors.'

At the time of the RTZ's AGM in 1997, campaigners wrote to the insurance companies that invest in the company urging them to raise their social and environmental concerns with RTZ's board, and to include ethical criteria in their decision-making. There are, however, problems with this. Many institutional shareholders are passive investors, preferring to raise issues privately rather than at AGMs. Even when resolutions are tabled, voting turnouts are often disappointing.

In a timely move, the President of the Board of Trade, Margaret Beckett, published the DTI's proposals for the review of company law, including reforms to promote transparent stewardship of investments and encourage the disclosure of voting policy and practice. Even without these improvements, the tactic of targeting institutional shareholders resulted in RTZ making an improved offer of compensation to the Amungme tribe and adopting a new community development policy. This has been rejected by the Amungme, but does represent a step towards agreement.

The continuing campaign
At WDM we are arguing that multinational companies must ensure that they have the prior informed consent of local communities

before they commence operations: be it RTZ in West Papua, Shell in Ogoniland, Nigeria, or P&O in the 'lungs of Bombay' in the Dahanu region of India. In addition, we are pressing for multi-nationals to both respect workers' rights and ensure that consumers don't get a raw – and hazardous – deal, by, for example, selling medicines and pesticides in the Third World which have long been banned elsewhere.

Whilst voluntary agreements and codes of conduct have been forthcoming after pressure from campaigners (in the Asian toy industry, for example, or between Del Monte and a banana workers' trade union in Costa Rica), these are nowhere near far-reaching enough and greater regulation of multinationals is going to be needed. The debate now is about just how to do this: at what level and using which institutions.

In essence, as far as multinationals are concerned, it is a question of maximizing the benefits and minimizing the costs – putting people before profits – and that very often means putting place before profits too. Place is particularly important for people living in developing countries, as it is often linked so directly to livelihood. But it's important to us in industrialized countries too. From the swans at the foot of Twyford Down to the sacred mountain of West Papua, a sense of connection to locality links people, especially when it is under threat. It is then that you realize just how important it is.

Converging Upon the Local

Dr Mark Redman

Research Fellow and Independent Consultant,
Centre for Land-Based Studies, Bournemouth University

My central theme is convergence, beginning with the convergence of personal conviction and professional perspective that has led me to value a personal characteristic that I spent years trying to shed – the fact that I am a 'local'. I am the product of a locality, and a tiny part of that locality is now inevitably and irretrievably the product of me.

I come from a small community in North Dorset where my family have lived for generations. A place that frustrated me for years with what I perceived as narrow-minded provincialism; a place that I, along with many of my peers, turned our backs on in our late teens and left – never intending to return. It is a place now that infuses me with a profound sense of familiarity and belonging – a place to which my wife and I chose to return to raise our own children. It is a place that is now not just my home, but part of my professional arena – a place that I have come to love for its humble complexity, its multiplicity of nuance, its many imperfections and the glorious and simple reality that it frames all aspects of my life within.

Positive parochialism
This may seem a distinctly parochial perspective - and of course it is. But I am not a rural xenophobe; I am simply offering my own

expression, my own experience of 'positive parochialism' – a term coined by Common Ground – that has infected me and is bubbling to the surface of communities around the globe.

Positive parochialism is not simply about sentimental attachments to what has been and what remains in our own localities. It is about pragmatism and the need to reappraise our own relationship with that tiny nook of the biosphere, that cranny of the global economy that we live our own small lives in. It is about the absolute necessity for us all to take more responsibility for our own locality as a fundamental step towards trying to improve humanity's prospects for achieving some form of socially and environmentally sustainable global development.

This may seem a rather dry analysis, but what is really inspiring is to see this positive parochialism emerging as simple intuition amongst individuals and communities who have no interest in rationalizing their own vision and commitment.

Local initiatives
In 1992 a small group of rural women in Lithuania came together to form an association around a common vision – a vision of an emergent democracy in which they were not disadvantaged by their rurality, by the residual reliance upon centralized bureaucracies, or by the entrenched perspectives of their men folk. They came together around the vision of a democracy that encompassed, celebrated and encouraged local distinctiveness and local action – with all of its attendant enterprises and endeavours – as the fundamental building block of their personal, communal and national identity. Today they have 2,000 members organized in 100 groups throughout Lithuania. They are now one of the largest and most active non-governmental organizations (NGOs) in the country with funding from the Lithuanian government, the US Agency for International Development and the European Commission. Why? Because their intuition converges precisely with international thinking on so-called 'sustainable development'.

The local and the global are at this moment converging in the villages and small towns of Lithuania. This convergence is not only bringing colour again to the local countryside, but it is injecting colour into the lives of countless grey men in grey suits in grey offices presiding over the grey detail of post-Communist reforms.

I have focused first on the rural women of Lithuania because I have the good fortune to work with them. My experience of the local has converged with theirs. But what is happening elsewhere and is it all so good?

One of the most exciting things to emerge from the Rio Earth Summit in 1992 is the way in which local authorities have embraced the concept of what is commonly known as Local Agenda 21 – and the way in which this is invigorating public participation in determining the future of local communities and their local environment. There is now a wonderful range of initiatives enabling local people to participate in practical action at a local level which aims to conserve resources, enhance biodiversity, promote primary healthcare and reinforce local distinctiveness.

Changing lifestyles

Important as these collective actions may be, there remain significant obstacles to moving the general populace towards the more fundamental changes of lifestyle that are required to forge a more sympathetic and more forgiving relationship with the natural world – changes in lifestyle that relate to the way we travel, what we eat, how we work, and where we spend our money.

Part of the problem is that people feel inconsequential in relation to the sheer magnitude of global problems. Simply informing people about the need to change their behaviour is unlikely to inspire action. All too often the state of our localities has deteriorated to such an extent that without significant intervention there are very few opportunities for local people to act sustainably. It is, for example, very difficult to encourage local people to use their cars less if local bus services have been cut or if the corner shop has been closed, and there are very few jobs within cycling distance.

If we are to promote a fundamental change in the lifestyle of the majority of people we must develop and then exploit a sense of 'enlightened self-interest'. We must make 'sustainable development' more of a quality of life issue, moving it away from the global arena to the local, where people can see, feel, smell and taste the success of their endeavours.

Agriculture and food
One of the most fundamental issues concerning our relationship to the local is the food we eat. Society as a whole has never been so separated from the natural world that sustains it with food. We have never been so isolated from the reality – and the consequences – of the decisions which are taken in our name as 'food consumers'.

There are alternatives to the present social and environmental impact of modern food production and distribution systems, to the continued absurdity of agricultural policies and to the folly of allowing greater and greater control of our food supply to accumulate in the hands of fewer and fewer people. There are many oases of enlightened self-interest in the agricultural community. There are farmers committed to working with, not against, nature, who see themselves as custodians, not agro-industrialists and who understand that ultimately their businesses can only be sustained by working within the capacity of local resources. They are building self-reliant and resilient production systems for the benefit of us all by maintaining, enhancing and restoring biological, economic and social diversity on their farms.

Through these farmers' diversity of practice and enterprise we can be connected to the land again. We can ask questions about where our food comes from or how far it has travelled from plough to plate. We can seek out good quality, affordable, locally produced food, preferably with the additional assurance that it is also organic. We can rekindle a sense of belonging to a locality and come closer to knowing the spirit of the place by eating food that has been grown and produced there.

We can converge upon the local again, and can all partake of the good living that is to be found there.

MOVING THE WORLD FORWARD

DEREK OSBORN, CB

Chairman, European Environment Agency and UNED/UK

The environmental race is a long-distance event in which victory depends on steady pacing and where friends and supporters help on the way. The prize, ultimately, is less significant to the participants than the fact of having taken part. The key element relevant to environmental activity is the concept of shared endeavour and how this can be strengthened and transmitted. The environment belongs to everyone; by the same token, it can be looked after only by collective action.

Local and international action
The environment can provide a rallying point and a focus of collective effort at all levels of activity, in the home and locality just as in the great issues of world politics. The great issues can inspire the small and local, and lend them significance. The small concerns can bring the global issues down to earth and anchor them in the realities and practicalities of everyday life.

I will focus here on the international level of activity and how to make that as effective as possible. This will only work if we can build and reinforce a sense of common purpose and transmit it to succeeding generations and champions. International action is absolutely necessary to make progress on the major global problems facing the world's environment such as global warming. There are other environmental problems which overlap national or regional boundaries where a common approach worldwide also makes for better progress than relying solely on national or local action. Equally, international agreements on subjects such as trade, investment or enforcement and policing need to take proper account of environmental objectives. The necessary political will cannot be generated for difficult policies unless there is a sense of shared endeavour and fair burden-sharing between the different parts of the world. So arrangements for development assistance and for encouraging or regulating international trade and investment also need to take proper account of the environment.

International advantages and failings
International meetings are crucial in building trust between nations and can be the forum for agreements on new international law. They can agree programmes of action and commitment of resources. They can enable participants to share knowledge, establish networks and forge new means for monitoring the effective implementation of environmental agreements. But international events can fail in as many ways as they succeed. Agreements can fail to materialize or be so limited as to be tantamount to failure. They can result not in the meeting of minds but in reinforcement of prejudices. No international conference or process ever has been a total success, but how can we get the best out of them?

Long-term objectives and clarity about the nature and function of individual meetings within a long-term strategy are important. It is surprising how casually some international meetings are set up, or for what irrelevant reasons of prestige or political kudos. It is wonderful to see how events can be moved forward by the determined leadership of a few, coupled with professionalism in running conferences. Clarity about the purpose of a meeting and its place in an evolving sequence of events helps towards clarity about getting the right participants with the right mandates. The participation of industry, non-governmental organizations (NGOs) and other groups in society is important. Increasingly they are involved within countries in shaping the environmental agenda. They need to be equally involved internationally.

It is also important to encourage professionalism and continuity. International processes and negotiations in the environmental field extend over many years. They are complex both in process and in substance. At present, many of those who have dominated the international environmental scene in the past are beginning to retire. Thus a new generation of champions inside and outside government are urgently required to learn the skills needed and to take up the environmental baton at international level.

Identifying tractability
Clear thinking and professionalism are necessary but not sufficient. Why are we able to make progress on some issues but not others? It depends on the level of tractability. An international environmental problem is tractable if it is capable of being brought to a successful outcome by an international process. Yet there are many issues of crucial importance which are highly intractable.

Features of a tractable environmental issue include:

- widespread understanding of the basic science and facts;
- a serious and clearly identified threat or risk if collective international action is not taken;
- a clear and accepted causal chain;
- feasibility of actions to eliminate or moderate the causes of the problem at acceptable economic cost;
- feasibility of establishing equitable burden-sharing to deal with the problem, particularly between North and South;
- practicability of implementation and enforcement.

In addition to these fundamental tractability requirements any successful process needs:

- active champions;

- sufficient time for preparation and negotiation;
- sufficient political focus and build-up in the media and local communities about the significance of the event;
- good rapport between individuals in the negotiations;
- common purpose within each principal country about the objectives – countries are often hamstrung by lack of unity at home and insufficient room for manoeuvre.

To identify how to make the most important issues more tractable over time, it is worth considering what have been good processes and what less good. The series of meetings from the late 1980s onward on the protection of the ozone layer fulfilled every one of the tractability criteria – or rather, over time it was made to fulfil them. There was good science and a clear health risk to stimulate public awareness; wealthy multinationals were an ideal target for action; and the problem did not have unmanageable North–South dimensions. In spite of these advantages the negotiations had their share of difficulties. They extended over a long period and were only brought to a comparatively successful position by the efforts of a number of individual champions, the establishment of a strong international network involving the worlds of government, business and NGOs, and continued media and public interest.

Climate change
Compare the tractability of the ozone layer issues with the difficulty of moving the climate change debate forward. The underlying science is still uncertain. The impact in different parts of the world is not clear. The causes are multiple and involve almost all human activity. The measures that might be taken to mitigate the causes are complex and politically and economically difficult. They raise acute problems of equity, particularly between North and South. Targets and measures to achieve them raise acute problems of implementation and enforcement. Nevertheless the perils of doing nothing are becoming steadily clearer, and some heavyweight political

champions are beginning to move the world forwards with substantive agreements on how to manage the problems.

Biodiversity scores badly on every one of the tractability tests and even lacks a single definition. Most of the concern about its loss is expressed in the North but most of the action would be needed in the South. There is little sign of sufficient resources coming from the North to back effective action. Concern about the world's forests and fresh water have not even reached the stage of international negotiations; by contrast, concerns about management of the oceans are almost buried by a multitude of overlapping agreements and interested organizations. Everywhere the story is worst of all when it comes to action programmes or agreements about the deployment of resources.

Against this background it is important to stress the significance of the kind of overview meeting represented by the Rio Earth Summit, the governing councils of the UN Environment Programme (UNEP) and the annual meetings of the UN Commission for Sustainable Development. These meetings shape agendas and priorities, and help to create conditions in which individual negotiations can prosper. They are opportunities for new issues to be identified and for new players to begin to make their mark. They can unblock institutional barriers or establish new institutional structures. They can institute long-term cooperative scientific or analytic work. They can engage the attention and participation of world industry and other major groups. They can be the occasion for major review of the balance of interests between North and South and the terms on which they can cooperate. Overview meetings are not themselves the occasion for detailed, hard negotiations but they can have a role in changing the climate and context of debate on particular problems. They can make the intractable tractable.

The 2002 Earth Summit
Now is the time to plan for the next great sustainable development summit envisaged for 2002. The Rio Earth Summit of 1992 helped

to advance the cause of sustainable development throughout the world. World leaders signed two major conventions on climate change and biodiversity. The Rio Declaration on Environment and Development proclaimed 27 Principles to guide sustainable development and Agenda 21 was adopted as a programme of action to implement these across the world. The issues put on the agenda in Rio are still the most powerful force in the global sustainable development agenda. Even so, progress is slow. The annual meetings of the UN Commission for Sustainable Development have had some success in maintaining pressure on particular issues. But they have not been able to halt the decline in overall levels of aid to the South, and the souring of North/South cooperation on sustainable development which was flowed from this.

The 2002 Earth Summit will be the biggest opportunity for a comprehensive effort to push forward the sustainable development agenda that is likely to arise within the next 10 years. It is a prime opportunity for a new generation of champions to push the agenda forward vigorously. Action is required to achieve effective political mobilization around the issues in all parts of the world involving all parts of society, linked with full-length international negotiations to define issues and bring them to a head.

The first step is the establishment of national coordinating groups or networks in interested countries to summarize and analyse key problems and objectives to be delivered internationally. Following informal soundings with various groups and individuals, United Nations Environment and Development/UK has recently taken steps to initiate a preparatory consultation on these lines. The first analysis will be used in 1999 to consult more widely in order to establish a broader basis of understanding and a consensus nationally and internationally on the issues which would be worth putting into formal negotiation in the years 2000 to 2002.

My provisional wishlist for elements we might hope to bring off at a 2002 environmental summit are:

- new forms of partnerships between countries of the North and South, both multinational and bilateral, and involving private and voluntary sectors as well as governments;
- new deals on development assistance and the channelling of private sector investment in more sustainable ways;
- making international agreements on trade and investment give better recognition to sustainable development;
- institutional agreements on how best to handle environmental and sustainable development issues at international level;
- better implementation and enforcement of international agreements;
- international recognition and support for the part played in sustainability by all major groups in society.

THE ENVIRONMENT'S FINANCIAL AND REGULATORY FRAMEWORK

HUGH RAVEN

Convenor, Government's Green Globe Task Force

T he UK played a leading role in the preparations for the Rio Summit in 1992, at the Rio conference itself, and in many of the international agreements both before and arising from Rio. It is worth emphasizing that the UK is extremely good at environmental diplomacy. We have an honourable tradition of it, with excellent legal and scientific teams in the Department of the Environment, Transport and Regions, and some very good and committed people in other departments too. It is a tradition which this government has been keen to build on – and, so far, not without achievement.

The Foreign Office and the environment
The Foreign Office's interest in the environment has increased sharply since the 1997 election, partly because Foreign Secretary Robin Cook has a long-standing commitment to environmental issues; and partly because there have been an unusually large number of international environmental events over the last few months. Amongst these have been the UN Special Session, where by universal consent Prime Minister Tony Blair made the most important contribution; the Commonwealth meeting, where the environment was on the agenda at the UK's behest; Kyoto, where

again the UK team led by John Prescott, Minister for the Environment, Transport and Regions, made the running; and the UK Presidency of the European Union, during which Robin Cook has ensured that the environment is one of the three main themes.

Levels of aid

Much progress on international environmental issues depends on finding causes which align the interests of North and South. The decline in overall levels of aid to the South has caused disillusionment in Southern countries at what they regard as broken promises by Northern countries about aid. Britain has dropped down the league table of donors, from fourth in absolute terms a few years ago to fifth in 1994 and sixth in 1998. Although we have a government pledged to increase the aid budget towards the UN's target figure of 0.7 per cent of gross national product from next year, that will be going against the international trend.

Many people despair that declining aid budgets spell declining commitment to development – and certainly reductions in aid are going to be very difficult to square with commitments entered into at Rio. But whether official flows continue to decline or again start to rise, they are eclipsed by the investment of private capital in developing countries.

Direct foreign investment

Direct foreign investment tends not to go to the poorest countries, and normal investment business will take some time to recover from turmoil in the Far East. Nevertheless, an increasing number of thinkers in the overseas development world – another area in which the UK has far more than its quota of expertise – are concentrating on influencing the quality of private investment rather than the amount of aid.

More direct foreign investment in developing countries is controlled from the City of London than from any other place on earth. Yet it is almost totally beyond the control or even influence of the global institutions which we have been talking about. Recent attempts by the Organization for Economic Cooperation and Development (OECD) to change that with the Multilateral Agreement on Investment have been unsuccessful. I suspect it will be many years before global institutions catch up with the globalization of finance and put in place an appropriate regulatory framework.

In the meantime we shall see investors taking a much greater interest themselves in the impact which their money is having overseas. With the rise of ethical investment, it will be individual investors, non-governmental organizations (NGOs) and the finance houses which start to ensure that private investment is contributing towards sustainable development in the South. I hope that official flows will increase, too, but the point is that it is ridiculous that only official flows should be considered legitimate when evaluating whether we have met our obligations to the South.

The corporate role
In 1998 Charles Handy predicted in the *Financial Times* that before long many state visits to the UK and similar countries would be carried out not by politicians or monarchs, but by chief executives. He invited his readers to 'picture the scene as Jack Welch, chairman of General Electric, steps off his aeroplane at Heathrow to be greeted by a guard of honour and God Save the Queen, to be whisked off to talks at Number 10'.

This is a prospect which appals many people in both the Labour Party and the voluntary sector. Personally, I am more relaxed about this scenario, for two main reasons. Firstly, because I don't think we can stop it, and the art of campaigning – or diplomacy, for that matter – is concentrating on those things which you can influence. Secondly because, as we have seen recently with some particularly enlightened corporate leadership, companies these days are much more responsive to the global challenges which used to be thought of as the exclusive preserve of governments.

Here again, Britain is in the lead. The series of speeches by John Browne, chief executive of BP, on the responsibility of corporations in areas such as climate change and human rights were of huge significance. He is the exception. For every John Browne there are several Lee Raymonds – the chief executive of Exxon Oil, who went round the world before Kyoto predicting the direst fate for even the world's richest countries if a meaningful deal was struck to limit the burning of fossil fuels. For long-term business prospects and ability to recruit and motivate staff, I know which company I would choose if I were a potential investor.

My point here is that the next generation of negotiators will include not just governmental representatives and, increasingly, NGOs – as we saw at Rio and Kyoto – but also business representatives. For example, it will not be governments that work out the practical details of a carbon trading regime to allow the Kyoto targets to be met. It will be banks and oil companies.

International law

A third important issue is the susceptibility of many of the Multilateral Environmental Agreements, as the treaties are technically known, to be challenged under another body of international law, the General Agreement on Tariffs and Trade (GATT). We have lived with the risk of challenge for several years, and indeed some domestic environmental laws have already been ruled against under GATT, like the famous US tuna–dolphin case. But the incompatibility of the two bodies of law is getting more serious as more environmental agreements are struck, and as they become more important.

For the Kyoto agreement to result in meaningful cuts in carbon dioxide emissions will almost certainly require trading blocs to permit discrimination at their borders between goods according to whether they are produced in an energy-efficient way or not. This is against the terms of the GATT, and could easily be challenged, almost certainly successfully. Such a challenge would be a disaster for the global environment – and it could happen to a large number of other agreements and treaties, too.

Proposals for future action
We should aim to achieve compatibility between international laws on trade and the different set of laws on the environment. Progress on trying to amend international trade law to remove the incompatibility is stalled in the relevant committee of the World Trade Organization, mainly because less developed countries think that in that way lies hidden protectionism, and see no advantage for them in agreeing to any amendments. What they require – not unreasonably – is a *quid pro quo*, an agreement that if the North wants better environmental protection which might disadvantage the trading position of the South, then the South should get concessions on their concerns about aid.

To break the stalemate, concessions will have to be made. They could take the form of either greater access to developed country markets for exports from the poorest countries, the economic benefits of which could be far more important than a few percentage points on or off the aid budget; or they could take the form of new financial packages to help less developed countries on their path to sustainable development, such as large-scale private investment of Northern capital in renewable energy generation, mass rapid transit systems or clean production technologies.

This investment will necessarily be in the private sector, because only the private sector has sufficient funds to make this possible, and because most of the expertise in these areas is now found not in state research institutes but in private companies. These new investment vehicles will need to conform to agreed standards. If they are to adhere to these standards, there is no reason why they could not legitimately be counted as contributions towards the North's resource commitments to the South. From a business point of view, investment standards are very much in favour, as was clear in the very conception of the Multilateral

Agreement on Investment, itself the brainchild of international commerce.

Such a package would contain attractions for developing countries, which would receive more investment that conformed to basic sustainability criteria. It would appeal to business, which wants assurances that investment will not be subject to sudden new restrictions imposed by national governments. And it would breathe life into the stalled talks on resolving the incompatibility between international trade and international environmental laws. That would indeed be a fitting goal for the first years of the new millennium.

MILLENNIUM MINDSETS: REASONS TO BE CHEERFUL

JONATHON PORRITT

Director, Forum for the Future

Environmentalism and optimism are uneasy bedfellows. What possible grounds for optimism can there be when we are surrounded by an almost constant flow of bad news about the global or the local environment, when almost all the key indicators of planetary health are heading in the wrong direction? What's more, environmental optimists keep strange company. Should you ever find yourself in a room full of techno-fixers (who really do believe that there is a technological get-out to all our environmental dilemmas), platitudinizing Pollyannas ('I am sure it will all turn out for the best – and there are such a lot of trees in Amazon'), and out and out contrarians (for whom optimism is obligatory in all circumstances, whatever the scientific data may be telling us), you would quickly understand why pessimism remains the dominant mood among environmentalists intent on retaining their sanity.

It has been so since the moment Rachel Carson's book *Silent Spring* first had people reaching for their organic vegetables back in 1962. Playing a pessimistic hand served the environment movement well during that time, providing people with a powerful antidote to the remorselessly optimistic model of industrial progress that has dominated the last 40 years. Millions of concerned individuals have been sufficiently moved by those periodic blasts of prophetic doom and gloom to start making a difference in their own lives and pressuring politicians to follow suit.

However, things have moved on. The basic environmental case has been made and won. That was the single most important message to come out of the 1992 Rio Earth Summit. It's still taking politicians, business people and most of humanity an agonizingly long time to accommodate this new reality but it is happening. Year by year, the alternative model of genuinely sustainable progress makes a little headway, even when up against powerful backlashing.

Disempowering pessimism
Against that backdrop, ingrained and unresponsive pessimism is no longer an appropriate mindset. There is clear evidence that it now disempowers as many people as it stirs into action, and it has next to no impact on either politicians or the business community. Can-do mindsets, however, raise the possibility that the next generation of green activists will be calling at least as much on the resource of hopefulness in people as on the ever-lurking presence of despair.

Whilst it is essential to adopt rather more optimistic mindsets, they need to be both responsibly grounded (rooted in the reality of current patterns of ecological devastation) and carefully bounded (modest, often conditional, and different in tone and ideology from the mindless euphoria that most eco-optimists inflict upon us). Only then can environmental optimism have any claim to political legitimacy.

Here are six reasons to be cheerful that can inspire environmental optimism.

Science
First is the state of scientific knowledge. Part of today's crisis arises from our continuing reluctance as a species to be bound by the same laws of nature as constrain every other species. Laws of thermodynamics tell us that matter can be neither created nor destroyed, that nothing disappears, that everything has to go somewhere. The phenomenal reach and power of the Industrial Revolution has depended on successive generations systematically

denying that constraint, and on its leaders persuading their electorates that we are not bound by those laws.

Amazingly, at the eleventh hour, and ironically at the very moment when scientists have lost the trustworthiness and authority once taken for granted, modern science is forcing contemporary politicians to relearn the immutability of those laws, pressing their tender little noses into the deeply unpleasant errors of their predecessors' ways. Contaminated land, climate change, species extinction, soil erosion, deforestation, over-fishing – on all these issues, the quality and the depth of scientific data available to politicians is of a different order of magnitude to what was available to earlier generations.

It's slowly having an effect. There is a moment in most international environmental conferences when the scientists wind up their own deliberations and hand over to the politicians, leaving them with less room for the kind of equivocation and vested interest-mongering that served them so well in the past.

Technology
My second reason for optimism is technology. As an erstwhile castigator of techno-fixers this one doesn't come easily for me, but again, things have moved on. All the best techno-fixers today would seem to be dyed in the wool greenies. Check the credentials of international figures such as Amory Lovins (see page 107) and Ernst von Weizsacker and you will see how the environment movement has learned to play (and I would argue beat) the technology establishment at its own game.

With one or two exceptions – including genetic engineering and an exhumed nuclear industry – all the best technological shows in town are either greenish (energy efficiency, alternative fuels, integrated pest management) – or deeply green (solar power, fuel cells, organic agriculture). We may still have reservations, but to be able to play the technological progress card offers advantages to those intent on working with the grain of the human psyche rather than against it.

Agency

The word 'agency' is my third reason for optimism. When I started out 25 years ago, the environment was the domain of signed-up environmentalists, pioneering academics, a few reluctant politicians and an even smaller number of media types. Today the environment involves just about everybody and the great surge of energy that made the 1992 Earth Summit a ground-breaking event came in no small measure from that almost anarchic diffusion of the environmental agenda.

Forum for the Future is one direct consequence of that diffusion. We exist specifically to work with people in other sectors – in business, local government, professional associations and higher education in particular. The voluntary sector is still at the heart of the sustainability revolution rumbling away in contemporary society, but it is no longer the sole driving force.

There are dilemmas involved in working with other sectors, especially business. Systems of so-called wealth creation, in terms of profitability, earnings per share and so on, are rarely compatible with sustaining the sources of that wealth in terms of the human, social and ecological capital that underpin the dynamism of the global economy. On the other hand, more and more business people share that perspective, and a somewhat smaller number are seriously involved in trying to do something about it. The Forum's purpose is to encourage those business leaders through working partnerships, rather than hammering away at the rump of incorrigibles whose days are numbered anyway.

Policy

This is the fourth reason to be cheerful. Although I have criticised politicians, those who look back over the last 25 years will have few illusions about the depth of the contribution made by political leaders apart from the Green Party and the Liberal Democrats. The point is politicians don't have to lead; they just have to allow themselves to be led – by public opinion, by science, by opportunity, by expedience and, of course, by votes. The good news is that this is now happening. Compare the manifestos of the three major parties from 1979 to 1997. Our political élites are getting the message, often grudgingly, often incompletely, but incrementally.

Community
Community is a rather touchy-feely reason to be cheerful, but the resurgence of community interests is one of the most significant reinforcers of sustainability mindsets in contemporary Britain. Sustainable development and community participation must go hand in hand. You can dress up all sorts of useful things at the local level in the trappings of sustainable development, but unless those useful things are rooted in and permanently nurtured by their host communities they simply won't deliver the long-term environmental or social dividends now available to us.

For many local councillors and government officials this is proving to be a harder pill to swallow than they ever imagined. Local Agenda 21, the all-encompassing framework for making sustainable development operational at the local level, specifically requires authorities to consult and to reach consensus on what local people want.

This emerging mutuality of interest is heartening. Amitai Etzioni points out that for many years the environment movement and what he calls the communitarian movement have moved forward in parallel but have rarely converged. Many community activists saw environmentalists self-indulgently exercising their privilege of concern for the natural world, while many environ-mentalists couldn't understand why community activists appeared not to give a stuff for their all-important environmental causes.

If nothing else, the debate about what sustainable development means has narrowed that gap. It's not just community participation that walks hand in hand with sustainable development but social justice too. Nowhere has this found more powerful expression than in the Real World Coalition, which brings together organizations like the Worldwide Fund for Nature and Friends of the Earth with the Poverty Alliance, Save the Children, the Quakers and a host of groups working at community level to improve people's lives.

Spirituality

My sixth reason for optimism is spirituality. On a bright day, unconstrained by the dead hands of atheism, scientific materialism or the kind of evangelical fundamentalism that perversely sees the benignly muddled spiritual aspirations of the New Age as more worrying than having no such aspirations at all, I feel the undertow of earth-friendly values, ethics and beliefs growing in strength all the time. Indeed, it is potentially more powerful than all my other five reasons to be cheerful put together.

This is a process that has been going on ever since the Apollo space missions revealed the earth to us properly for the first time. To be in awe of the beauty and mystery of the planets, to feel connected to all other life forms on this planet, to celebrate the evolutionary journey that makes us what we are today after 4.5 billion years, to worship God in honouring that creation – there are more ways of opening up to those values, ethics and beliefs than any primer on the environment could ever tell you. Moreover, there are more people doing exactly that than any opinion poll, survey or wretched focus group will ever reveal.

These are six reasons to be cheerful, unencumbered by the usual battery of caveats and conditions without which even the most optimistic of environmentalists feels naked. I have not forgotten China, the insanity of exponential economic growth, endocrine disruption, the endemic corruption in Indonesia, the daily death of 37,000 children under the age of five from preventable diseases, the 328 billionaires whose net wealth is equal to that of the poorest two billion human beings on earth today, the amoral capacity of global capitalism and so on. I have just set them to one side before they come thundering back as so many irrepressible conscripts in the cavalry of the Apocalypse.

FACING THE ENVIRONMENTAL CHALLENGES

JULIE HIRIGOYEN

Analyst, Environmental Governance;
Former Forum for the Future Scholar

A s a Forum for the Future Scholar, and as an ardent believer in the powerful language of 'sustainable development', it would be hypocrisy for me to paint a picture of doom and gloom for the future of our planet. I, too, believe in Jonathon's 'reasons to be cheerful' (see pages 39 to 45) and I too have seen enormous efforts being made by inspired individuals in various sectors of society to instigate the change which is currently essential.

However, despite my strong conviction that there must be solutions to the environmental crisis which we face, I do not believe that an easy task lies ahead, either to identify or to implement these solutions. Looking forward into the twenty-first century I see a multitude of challenges, and in order to succeed in overcoming these, it is vital that we first understand the driving forces behind them. It is these challenges that I wish to focus on: aspects of tomorrow's world which will need to be addressed before we can truly live in a sustainable society. These can be clustered into four separate categories: global, national, local and personal.

Global challenges

At a global level, the population growth rate is such that approximately 94 million additional people come onto the planet

every year. The worst case scenario put forward by the UN projects
that the entire global population will almost double from the
current 6 billion to a staggering 11.9 billion by the year 2050.

Population growth is inevitably a strain on natural resources.
More people implies the clearing of more forests, the depletion of
ever increasing quantities of groundwater and the consumption of
more and more energy, all of which could spell ecological disaster
for the planet. But the irony lies in the fact that it is the industrialized North, with its low population growth and its obscene
patterns of over-consumption, that is responsible for the vast
majority of global environmental impacts. Statistics suggest that
between 80 and 90 per cent of the world's environmental resources
are consumed by about 20 per cent of its population living in
industrial countries.

However, with rapid globalization and the infiltration of
Northern ideals into every country of the world, we now face the
problem of less developed countries aspiring to consume as much
as we do. Asia provides the perfect example: its economy is
booming, but due to a lack of concern for the environmental
implications, Asian industrialism will soon be to blame for an
ecological catastrophe. And yet who are we to try and stop it?

The final – and particularly salient – challenge in the global
context is the failure of our global institutions to deliver on the
environment. The United Nations Environment Programme is
riddled with management problems and characterized by a lack of
resources. The World Bank is above all else a bureaucratic
institution which has a historically bad reputation for releasing
funds for inappropriate mega-projects in the pretext of reducing
poverty. And last, but by no means least, the establishment of the
World Trade Organization seems set to ensure that trade will
always get precedence over the environment in international
negotiations, as exemplified by the Organization for Economic
Cooperation and Development's Multilateral Agreement on
Investment.

National challenges

Turning now to the national level, whispers about sustainable development may be heard throughout the corridors of Whitehall, but nothing refutes the fact that today's political machine is built upon short-termism. Politicians are not yet foolish enough to introduce suicidal policies which result in long-term benefits for future generations and simultaneous loss of office. Now that environmentalism has recognized the urgent need to incorporate social justice issues within its remit, it requires distributional measures of the kind to make even politicians blush! For a government which pledged to become 'the first truly green government ever', the Budget has been disappointingly weak with respect to ecotaxation.

Talking at a national level also begs the question of what the nations of the next century actually are. Are they individual political states such as France, or newly devolved mini-states such as Scotland? Are they collective super-states such as the European Community, or indeed are they not the borderless super-powers to whom we bow today – the multi-national corporations whose activities are global and whose cash flows remain unchecked? Is it not they who are setting the agenda for Tomorrow's World?

The Kyoto Climate Summit in December 1997 illustrates this. Despite being faced with terrifying scenarios on global climate change, the United States (and other nations) could not bring themselves to make industry suffer for purely environmental concerns. The question is would they have acted differently if they could be held accountable for the widespread devastation which California, and other areas, have since suffered in the face of El Niño?

Local challenges

It is my belief that, in order to succeed, it is crucial for sustainability to begin on a small, local scale, reflecting the needs and desires of the community. In theory, therefore, local authorities should be ideally suited to steering communities towards a more sustainable way of life. In practice, this is proving to be a trying and difficult challenge for them.

Local Agenda 21 (LA21), which came out of the Rio Earth Summit in 1992, is the vehicle by which local councils can deliver sustainable development to their communities. However, by virtue of being a non-statutory obligation, and in light of the sobering cuts in central government grants in recent times, LA21 is all too frequently interpreted by local authorities as an additional area of work which officers have neither the skills nor the time to undertake. Looking into the future, this challenge will no doubt be compounded by the Regional Development Agencies, whose legislative duties regarding economic development are stringent, but whose role in ensuring that this development be sustainable is weakly provided for in the policy to date. Besides, the further local governance distances itself from the people themselves, the less likely is the possibility of delivering a just and equitable sustainability agenda for all.

Community participation and involvement is a crucial component of Local Agenda 21, and one which is all too often overlooked. Giving people voices, and empowering them to participate in the decisions which affect them, is not a process with which politicians or decision-makers are yet comfortable. There are no formal constitutional mechanisms for community development, and the truth is that people themselves may not yet be ready for such radical changes.

People are frequently cynical when they talk of local councils, and traditional distrust may all too often replace cooperation. I wonder how different this might be if our engine of democracy were more efficient than today. Indeed, the pitifully low turnout at local elections means that councillors can never be truly representative of their local communities.

Personal challenges
Finally, there is a need to focus on the personal challenges which we face as individuals, for, in a sense, society is only what we make of it, and if we were all to accept our responsibilities to each other and

to our life support systems, there would no longer be an environmental crisis. So what is it that stops us from doing so?

I believe it is a question of morals and ethics, and that those which underpin our current society are too removed from the natural world to recognize its inherent value. Children today grow up learning about the environment and about the dangers facing planet Earth. But how much of this message is genuinely reflected in the television programmes they watch, the computer games which they play, or the cyberpets which they adopt? It is as though material things have taken over from more complicated feelings and emotions, and humanity has lost touch with the very reason it exists.

It is this change in ideology that represents the greatest challenge of all. And it *is* a personal challenge, because at the end of the day we are all to blame for the consequences of our actions. We are all consumers; we all purchase goods every day without knowing who produced them and how, what distance they have travelled to get to us, and what will be done with them once we have thrown them away. Each and every one of us is capable of making a difference through the daily choices and decisions we make. The crucial challenge then, is for us to be aware of this and to accept the responsibilities which we have towards the planet, each other and generations to come. It is all too easy to blame the system for not delivering, but it becomes unfair when we, as the people who shape society, do nothing at all to steer it in a better direction.

Unprecedented opportunities

In conclusion, it is important to emphasize that although the twenty-first century poses several challenges, it also offers many more opportunities than the environmental movement has ever before been able to enjoy. Despite having sounded a little less cheerful than Jonathon Porritt, I am not less optimistic, for I strongly believe that something can be done to overcome the challenges. I only hope that those of us working to promote sustainable development in all sectors of society live to see our efforts rewarded by solutions to the difficulties which I have talked about.

THE NEXT GENERATION OF ENVIRONMENTALISTS

GUY THOMPSON

*Parliamentary Officer, Royal Society for the Protection of Birds;
Former Forum for the Future Scholar*

What are the grounds for optimism within the next generation of environmentalists? What exactly is there for us to be cheerful about on the verge of the next Millennium? I shall posit two optimist theories about the future of environmentalism to illustrate how a constructive outlook could be a driving force for real change.

The next generation of environmentalists
My first point is that the next generation of environmentalists will be wholly unrecognizable from the original movement represented by Jonathon Porritt and his contemporaries. The environment is no longer the sole preserve of biologists and conservationists. Advocates of sustainable development, as distinct from the environmentalism of old, can be found throughout society. I have only recently escaped from the voluntary environmental sector, but I don't see myself as an environmentalist. I certainly hold strong ethical beliefs that we should be better at protecting our natural environment, but I further believe that sustainable development pervades aspects of society traditionally seen as irrelevant to environmentalists. Sustainable development is becoming an increasingly important concept to all sectors of society. That is one reason for being cautiously optimistic about the future.

So the next generation of environmentalists will not be known as such. We will soon all need to be environmentalists. My generation has seen a growing awareness of the vulnerability of our global environment. We grew up watching Jonathon Porritt on *Going Live* on Saturday morning television; we grew up with media stories about the depletion of the ozone layer and global warming – incontrovertible evidence that man *is* having a damaging impact upon the Earth. My generation can no longer have faith in the ability of the natural environment to sustain our current way of life.

All this means that environmental awareness must be at unprecedented levels amongst the youngest generations. There is little empirical evidence that I can use to support this argument. But, by way of example, it has been noticeable that as the Forum for the Future Scholars progress through the various sectors on work placement, it is invariably the youngest employees of our host organizations who exhibit the highest levels of environmental awareness and the greatest capacity to take on new ideas. The next generation is therefore inherently comprised of environmentalists and it is our responsibility to carry this into our careers and everyday lives.

The latent potential of sustainable development
My second contention is that as the environmental movement broadens to incorporate sustainable development, with its triple bottom line (economic prosperity, environmental quality and social equity), it will become a more potent force for change within society. We may joke about the popular perception of biodiversity as a brand of washing powder but when people are asked about the green spaces around them and their day-to-day concerns about quality of life, it is clear that they do care about their environment.

It matters to people because it touches upon their everyday lifestyles. The global environment, with all its intangibles, translates neatly into the local environment, where the issues can be seen for real. For example, traffic congestion and the health effects of pollution are of greater concern at a local level than the Greenhouse Effect, but they are all symptoms of the same problem. The new environmentalism – the language of sustainable development – therefore has powerful potential for addressing the everyday needs of local communities. Sustainable development pervades all aspects of our modern lifestyle and, as such, is now a real driving force for change.

In response to the challenges that Julie Hirigoyen outlined (see pages 47–51) I will now highlight a few of the opportunities that lie ahead for the environmental movement at different levels.

Global perspective

At a global level, the shift towards a free world trade order is inexorable, but this is underpinned by international consensus on the need for action on key global problems. As Jonathon Porritt has already pointed out (see pages 40–44), the last ten years have seen unprecedented levels of international cooperation on the environment. The UN Earth Summit at Rio in 1992 was a ground-breaking event, which played a key role in achieving this consensus. The debate about the need for a new global environment agency to replace the beleaguered United Nations Environment Programme (UNEP) is in fact taking place only as a result of the Programme's past successes. UNEP has spawned international treaties with their own secretariats. The number of environmental staff at institutions such as the World Bank has increased vastly over the last decade. UNEP has simply become less relevant within the context of changing priorities in modern international relations.

The very fact that a deal was secured at the Kyoto Climate Convention is grounds for optimism in itself. This represents the first legally binding agreement for international action on an environmental issue ever. My first work placement on the Forum for the Future Scholarship Programme was at Greenpeace during the run-up to Kyoto. At that time, they were busily preparing a PR strategy, in the apparent certain knowledge that the talks would end in collapse. And yet a deal was done. I have no doubt that many environmental groups who were publicly critical of Kyoto were privately amazed that a deal was secured at all.

National perspective

Time will tell whether Tony Blair's government will indeed become 'the first truly green government ever'. It has unquestionably made some important progress in government so far. With the benefit of a recent placement inside the Labour Party headquarters, I see this as falling into three distinct areas.

First, there have been some major structural changes at the heart of government. We have a new Cabinet Committee on the Environment and a new super-ministry in the form of the Department of the Environment, Transport and the Regions. These changes have been expressly made in order to better integrate environmental considerations into the policy-making process. This is the first time that it could ever be argued that the environment has been included in a UK government's strategic priorities.

Secondly, the Government has been taking a lead on the international environmental stage. The important role played by John Prescott at Kyoto is a case in point. And, thirdly, there are some exciting new policy initiatives taking place, such as the Transport White Paper.

These developments do seem to point to a broad groundswell of change in British politics. It is increasingly recognized that environmental issues pervade all areas of government, at both national and local levels. This dictates the need for a more integrated approach to policy-making that allows for cross-compliance between traditional areas of departmental jurisdiction. Tony Blair has frequently alluded to a new consensus in British politics and has stated his aim of bringing about a new style of governance in Whitehall. It could be argued that sustainable development would provide the ideal foundation for such a consensus, touching as it does on social, economic and environmental policy dimensions. The most significant progress towards sustainable development, however, will be made within civil society, through strategic alliances between different sectors. There is certainly a limit as to how much of the sustainable development agenda can be achieved by national governments alone.

Local perspective

The message of the Rio Earth Summit was to 'think global and act local'. Despite Julie Hirigoyen's concerns, the Local Agenda 21 process *is* quietly revolutionizing the approach of many UK local authorities to environmental and social issues. It has been inspiring to see the levels of energy and commitment being put into making this work in some authorities. Even more encouraging, Tony Blair has now signalled the Government's intention that all authorities should have a Local Agenda 21 strategy by the year 2000.

It is only through the empowerment of local communities that environmental concerns can be acted upon. Despite its teething difficulties, Local Agenda 21 is proving to be an effective mechanism for achieving this. Whether it likes it or not, local government is having to reconcile itself with a cultural change in the way that it consults and involves communities. Although we are living in a global world, the role of local government is crucial to the sustainable development agenda, and we are already seeing trends move in the right direction.

The role of partnerships

Progress in all of these areas shares a common theme – that of partnership. New forms of partnership are evolving in every sector of the economy, involving complex mixtures of government and non-governmental, business and other agents. Environmentalists today recognize that nothing can be achieved within a policy vacuum. For example, Greenpeace attracted a capacity audience for its first business conference in September 1996. Some traditional environmentalists may have questioned what was going on, but the event was symptomatic of a significant mindshift that has taken place to transform relations between campaigning environmental organizations and business. And it is only through stakeholder partnerships such as these that sustainable development can truly have the impact on society that environmentalists advocate.

An instrument of change

Sustainable development is about finding a lifestyle that does not compromise the ability of future generations to meet their own needs. Engendering a constructive spirit of optimism about our future is therefore critical to its success. The role of the environmental movement is shifting from one of highlighting problems to one of identifying and promoting solutions in the search for a more sustainable and just way of life. In this way, the emergence of the sustainable development concept could see the popular perception of environmentalism shift from being seen as a barrier to change to an instrument of such change. And if this is so, we should all have cause to feel cheerful about our future as we begin the new millennium.

CHILDREN: ACTIVE CITIZENS FOR THE NEXT MILLENNIUM

The Save the Children/RSA Millennium Lecture
in Memory of Nicholas Hinton, CBE

PROFESSOR VITIT MUNTARBHORN

Faculty of Law, Chulalongkorn University, Bangkok

I have always felt that it is presumptuous to talk about children because they should really be allowed to talk about themselves. Children participate every day in one way or another. Recently a little boy won an award in Thailand because he was helping to feed his blind mother. Does it happen in Britain? Of course it does; one report of the Save the Children Fund (1996) says that 40,000 young people care for others in Britain, even though they might not have any help at all from the state. They might be fearful of seeking help because they may themselves end up in 'care'.

There is also a negative type of participation. Young boys, sometimes young girls, are pressed by various circumstances to carry out certain misdeeds. In the United States recently two young boys went on a shooting spree – but this is not the real kind of participation that I am talking about. I shall be looking at it from the angle of children as positive, active citizens for the new millennium.

Four major concerns
I would like to share four major concerns with you. One is my own personal concern. The second is conceptual. The third is institutional

– by the fact that all countries but two are now parties to a global institution known as the United Nations Convention on the Rights of the Child (CRC), an international treaty which sets down various key principles, including child participation and respect for the views of the child. Finally there is the experiential side: I will describe some projects from which we can learn for the future.

Participation for prevention

Child participation helps to prevent problems. If we spread information about AIDS to children, we can help to prevent AIDS. If we spread information about nutrition, health, good food, rest, through the children themselves, they can help to prevent problems every day – not only their problems but our problems.

Children can be very good at protecting other children and adults too. The 40,000 children caring for others in Britain are providing services, care and remedies. Child participation is very much an entry point to our understanding of child rights, children's entitlements, human rights, democracy, peace, development, environmental protection and so on. Globally we have come to accept that respect for the views of the child and child participation are a right, particularly under the CRC. It is not a matter of discretion, something for us to accord to children or not; it is a right to which they are entitled, as promised by all of our governments under the CRC.

Personal concern

I was sent to boarding school at the age of eight and remained there for ten years. I always felt that I was strange in the sense that I was non-conformist. I never liked the rules and I never liked to be told to go and play sports every afternoon. I couldn't understand it; I liked to go to the library or go and sculpt. But since I left boarding school I have become a great sports enthusiast because I have not been told to play sports.

Boarding school taught me that as an alternative to all the rules that I didn't quite understand there was one option that taught me a lot, and it is the root cause of what I am today. There was an activity known as voluntary service or community work. I chose to bike about once a week to visit an elderly citizen and do her gardening. I learnt to share my feelings for other human beings by doing the gardening. From that seminal experience I learnt to value the interaction via voluntary service and community service in sharing and caring for others. The dear lady always responded as best she could, because she was old and she couldn't go out very much. After the gardening she would give me tea and soggy biscuits, which I enjoyed – sogginess should not and does not dampen spiritual rejuvenation.

When I returned to Thailand some 18 years ago I started to become interested in community work, not because I initiated it but because my students did. They asked me to go and do community work with them in rural Thailand, particularly the eastern part which is very dry and arid. The first project we undertook was to build a library in north-eastern Thailand. There was no water, no electricity, and not much food, but we built it.

Something I learnt from the villagers was that even though they had very little to offer, they offered us almost everything they had. In the house where I stayed, which was built on stilts, all the family had to offer was the floor for me to sleep on (though that's the traditional Thai style), the mat which they had woven and the pillow which they had also made. When we had finished the construction and were on the point of departing, the family gave me the mat and the pillow. It dawned on me that while my students and I thought presumptuously that we were going out there to develop the villagers, I was the one who was developed, spiritually, by those who had so little.

That was really the beginning of my involvement in human rights issues, child rights and so on. I have continued to work particularly on literacy programmes, ultimately to concentrate more on child rights issues.

Conceptual concern

From the conceptual angle there is a lot of tokenism, a lot of decoration, a lot of manipulation that is not really participation of children. Sometimes adults use children for their own ends. Sometimes they think they are helping children when in fact it is mere decoration, such as giving the child a T-shirt about the environment but not really conveying the message or discussing it with the child. Or perhaps a conference is organized and children are asked to come, but they are insufficiently briefed beforehand and are not consulted properly about the conference. They come and make a little speech or wave their hands and have photos taken, but nothing is followed up. It is mere tokenism.

Conceptually, we can be more positive about child participation. If children are assigned to do things they must be fully informed. If, at the World Summit for Children in 1990, the children did not have a very loud voice, they were at least given a certain role which they understood, such as showing the leaders to their seats. We can consult children from the start. Even though they might not make the ultimate decisions, we can at least enable them to understand and enable them to be informed.

Ultimately there are three preferred types of participation. One is adult-initiated but decisions are shared with children; this could be an environment project with the children helping to implement it. Another is participation through a project being initiated, directed and implemented by children. The third type could be a child-initiated project with the decisions shared with adults. Academics disagree about which is the best choice. As a lawyer I would say the answer is a relative one: it depends on the different situations in which these three possibilities may be offered as options.

Children's participation as active citizens to me means treating children as citizens even if they don't have national, legal citizenship (though of course they should not participate in activities which are in breach of child rights or are detrimental to their development, such as child prostitution). That's the crunch, because in many contexts non-nationals, migrant workers and ethnic groups who don't have nationality are marginalized and not enabled to participate fully. In practice we have some hard choices. A newspaper reported that a Bangkok governor was campaigning to have his workers, including children, elected as part of a team in the municipality. Is this tokenism or not? Thai children are claiming that police assaulted them. Children are participating as advocates, as claimants, but who is protecting them when the formal institutions of many of our societies don't, and are sometimes actually the transgressors?

Culture, family and community need to be catalysed to work more with child participation. One also has to be realistic about the issue of paternalism in many of our societies. We don't just need laws; we need to look beyond. We need social mobilization and education to change old habits. We need good examples, good parents and good teachers, as peer pressure for change towards greater child participation.

Institutional concern
The third concern is institutional. One key principle of the international framework for child rights, the Convention on the Rights of the Child (CRC), to which Britain and Thailand are parties, is non-discrimination. This relates to the rights of all children in any country irrespective of whether they have that country's nationality. That is what child rights are about, and human rights as whole. A second principle, the best interests of the child, is a principle of our courts and we have to interpret it as best we can, without being paternalistic. A third is the right to life, survival and development. A fourth, and the one with which we are most concerned here, is respect for the child's views. This underlying principle affects everything. It means the right to express views freely in all matters affecting the child, and it means giving the views of the child due weight in accordance with age and maturity,

though respect for these views does not necessarily mean decision-making totally by the child.

There are many other principles and rights that ensue from that general principle under the Convention: freedom of expression; freedom of thought, conscience and religion, subject to appropriate parental guidance; freedom of association; access to information; right to education; right to leisure and recreation; and principles relating to difficult cases such as deciding on the level of participation for children in conflict with the law.

To date some 80 countries have been considered and analysed by an international committee established by the CRC to see how countries are performing in their implementation of child rights at national level. They include the United Kingdom; Thailand will be considered in September. What information can we get from these countries about child participation? Where is it most prominent and where is it least prominent?

There is one very simple conclusion. Through the 80 countries there is a high level of acceptance as regards child participation in decision-making concerned with recreation and leisure, and quite a lot of acceptance in relation to decision-making about family matters and adoptions – at least in legal terms, though in practice it might be a myth. There is much less information and less activity in the area of child participation of non-nationals, for example refugees or marginalized children such as migrants and minorities.

I looked at 70 of the 80 country reports and found that only about 25 gave concrete information on child participation. This is not much in terms of intention, let alone practice. In Chile, Mexico, Belgium, Bulgaria, Croatia, China and Nepal the constitution supports child participation on family-related matters and consultation over adoption. The Thai constitution includes it; Britain, of course, has no written constitution. Other countries which give relatively concrete information on child participation include Colombia, Namibia, Romania, Cyprus, Denmark, El Salvador, Ethiopia, Finland, Iceland, Madagascar,

New Zealand, Nigeria, the Philippines, Russia, Sweden and Tunisia.

Where there is substantial reference to child participation in the reports, much of it relates to recreation and culture. Namibia is introducing Youth Resource Centres which will look at after-school recreation, drama, life skills, counselling, career guidance; it will promote cultural clubs. Pakistan has Children's Palaces for after-school activities, Belarus has Palaces of Culture, Bulgaria has a National Palace for Children and China has Youth Palaces. Canada has a Commonwealth Youth Programme. Croatia has art workshops, environmentalist patrols, modelling workshops, musical workshops, an SOS Home for Children, Scouts, puppet theatre. There are schemes in Denmark and play areas in Jamaica. New Zealand has Kiwi Sport, Sportfit, Firestone Fair Play, and very good Kiwi Able programmes for those with disabilities. Norway has youth clubs and organizations. Tunisia has a National Puppetry Centre. Vietnam has sports festivals. Zimbabwe has a mass games training programme.

There is quite a lot of recognition of child participation in family matters. The consent of the child (minimum ages vary between 10 and 15) is needed for adoption in Namibia, Romania, Belgium, Bulgaria, Croatia, El Salvador, Iceland, Korea, the Philippines and Spain. The child has the right to be heard in adoption proceedings in Ireland, Cyprus and Ethiopia; and in judicial or administrative proceedings in Colombia, Finland, Germany, Iceland, New Zealand, Britain and Canada.

A smaller-scale but very interesting offshoot is the role of youth and student councils, particularly at school and in municipalities, where the children can come together as a group to learn, to share, to say what they would like to see from school and from the community, particularly the municipality. Not many countries have this: Namibia, Romania, France, Paraguay – and Britain a little. At national level I was looking for a national youth council which gave youngsters the chance to participate in decision-making. Namibia intends to introduce a National Youth Council. Denmark has a project which involves children in local decision-making. There are youth projects with community work in France, New Zealand and Britain.

Particularly interesting phenomena are the children's parliaments in Slovenia, Senegal, Spain and Jamaica. Elected children are consulted and informed, and they can negotiate at municipal or parliamentary level. Slovenia established its children's parliament in the early 1990s, before the war in Yugoslavia. The first meeting, on the environment, was very accusatory, blaming adults for causing the environmental havoc. One girl from the group said that the children's parliament had no intention of attending tiresome meetings, particularly with adults. They formulated their requests and expected politicians to do their job and to report to the next children's parliament.

The second Slovenia children's parliament was on leisure time, the third on schools. The fourth, which was very interesting, was on non-violence. The children were having to grapple not just with adult transgressions but with what was happening in school. They had to face bullying and to find a way out for themselves and others. They called for cooperation with adults to protect even so-called bad children to ensure that there would be non-violence at school.

Children can never be truly informed or consulted, nor able to make decisions, unless they have access to information. Of the 70 countries I looked at, only Canada and Denmark talk very much about children's access and the right to information, but there are some interesting examples of child-related media. Namibia, Nepal and the former Yugoslavia have children's publications, Mongolia has radio and TV with and for children, Russia has a special news agency.

Many countries are still very uncomfortable about religion as a means of participation. The message from the CRC is that the child has the right to choose, though parents can give guidance in accordance with the child's capacity and maturity.

As mentioned earlier, the country reports are weakest in areas relating to non-nationals and marginalized children – girls, refugees, displaced persons, migrants, minorities, indigenous groups, children in care, children in the juvenile justice system, children with disabilities, abused and exploited children. What is their scope for participation? The CRC has indicated some directions. It identifies needs to foster fuller respect of the child's views, to eliminate corporal punishment (school discipline should be worked out with the child rather than imposed by adults), to improve the juvenile justice system and family procedures, to respect freedom of assembly, to promote freedom of religion, to have choice of education for ethnic groups, to disseminate the convention, to change traditional attitudes on child participation, and to have more information on the participation of non-nationals and marginalized children.

Learning from experience
Lastly there is the experiential dimension. We can learn from projects in which children are involved and in which they contribute to helping others as well as themselves. The Save the Children Fund has become more and more involved with child participation. One of its most interesting experiments is children's consultation at municipal level in Birmingham, Kirklees and London. It includes inter-ethnic and cross-cultural interchange. Bangladeshi children, consulted about what they would like for the future, said that they feared bullying and racism and wanted more space to play, more safety, and more bilingual workers who can work with them and cross the boundaries of ethnicity.

Unicef established an Internet site called Voices of Youth. The greatest number of hits was on child labour. That must have been in children's minds because of coverage in the Press, the global march against child labour in 1998, culminating in a march to Geneva, or the Oslo conference on child labour in 1997. The second-biggest number of hits was on children's rights. There wasn't much on the subject of girls or on non-violence. The children had some wonderful ideas, such as electronic participation in the global march on child labour (for example, counting each hit by children on the Internet as one mile contributing to the miles walked in the global march). They had other good suggestions such as sponsored walks, sponsored car washes, raising funds for children in the Third World, supporting a school in Pakistan, even sponsored silence.

Different projects around the world offer many chances to learn from experience. For example, there are many things to be improved in China, but I find its early childhood education a key entry point for child participation. In Malaysia there are good facilities for early childhood education in towns, but elsewhere it might not be so good. Children are left on their own or with neighbours, with no games and very few toys. In the city the facilities are much better. If children are activated from the start in a child-friendly manner, they can become greater learners later as well as greater contributors.

In Brunei I talked to rich children and asked them what they would like to do for the future and for others. They wanted more community service, learning from the community, visits to rural Thailand, more song contests, more games, more media for children, a ship where children could get together. The spirit, even among rich children, was often to learn and to share with those who were less fortunate.

In Thailand university students do a lot of literacy work, going out every year to offer rural people some non-formal education. A youth training programme for people of 17 to 25 on the CRC explored different methods of conveying information. The first thing everyone was asked to do was: 'Express yourself. What are your expectations? Put your card on the wall. Or if you don't want to write, draw it. Express yourself concerning your aspirations and expectations.' One participant made a poster about the CRC with poetry.

We hear sad stories about street children in Brazil, but what about the more positive side? Youngsters who belong to the street children movement are able, sometimes with the help of adults, to protect themselves and to show that they can contribute to the community. In one programme the children, helped by a street educator, staged a play on the streets to earn money to feed themselves. Street children from about six countries in Asia attended a preparatory meeting to send their voices to the child labour conference held in Oslo in 1997. They made their own recommendations. They will not accept child labour in an intolerable or unacceptable form, such as child prostitution and child soldiering. They conveyed their hopes – and fears sometimes – through pictures, and ultimately by staging a play about the bad side of labour and what they would like to see for the future. The message was taken to Norway and influenced the Oslo declaration and plan of action on child labour (the Agenda for Action of the Oslo conference on child labour).

Orientations for the future
In conclusion I will highlight the orientations we need for the future if we are to ensure the participation of children as active citizens for the new millennium:

- more doing by example rather than preaching;
- more child participation from planning to implementation, evaluation and reform;
- more inter-child and youth cross-cultural interaction, particularly to promote understanding between ethnic groups;
- more community work, particularly to foster social consciousness;
- more child-to-child or youth–child links for peer education;

- more partnership building, between child and youth and youth and adult, for adequacy and implementation of child rights;
- more child participation pre-school, school, and after;
- more links between children in formal education and those who are out of school;
- more access to education for all;
- rest, leisure and recreation as entry points;
- charitable actions;
- child rights dissemination;
- community work;
- advocacy of child rights;
- peer monitors;
- environmental programmes;
- self-discipline;
- access to catalyse local and national administrative organs;
- child media;
- associations of the young;
- the use of modern technology to forge links between children, while not forgetting traditional forms such as songs and mime.

Early in 1998 some sexually abused children assembled in Canada to call for more action to help those who are sexually abused. I end with the words of three of them:

> I can't read or write because you chose not to teach me. I didn't even know what a uterus was. People look at me and think I'm a prostitute, just a prostitute. I'm also a mum, a sister, a daughter. It's just safe talking here with others from the trade. Just as an alcoholic can help another alcoholic, youth can really help other youth with similar struggles. Suicide lines don't

know how to deal with the issue we deal with. They can't cope with our reality. The prostitutes in my country are very young and have no place to sleep. They sleep on the streets, and this is when the men take advantage of them and rape them.

I'm turned away by prostitute agencies. I'm turned away by the gay community. I'm turned away by my friends and family because I'm not only selling my body, but I'm a guy selling my body to guys. It's not fair. It's just as scary to think of young boys being equally vulnerable to commercial sexual exploitation.

It shouldn't be OK to beat us up just because we're prostitutes. Child and youth prostitution is a reflection of the disease in society's soul. Many of us disappear without a trace. No one knows what happens to us when we die. A child is murdered and no one cares because she is a prostitute. Society's hands are just as bloody as the guy who did it.[1]

Note
Nicholas Hinton was Director General of Save the Children from 1984 to 1995.

Reference
1   Youth Voices from the International Summit of Sexually Exploited Youth, Victoria, Canada, March, 1998.

VOLUNTEERING AND THE PROBLEM OF PAY

The Geraldine Aves Memorial Lecture

JOHN EDMONDS

General Secretary, GMB – Britain's General Union

Geraldine Aves is remembered for her contribution to the development of volunteering in Britain. She believed that volunteering can enrich people's lives by adding an extra dimension to the experience of education, employment and retirement. Indeed, her own life combined a commitment to voluntary work with the development of a fulfilling career as a high-flying public service employee.

Wasted ability
Other people are less successful at striking such an elegant balance between paid and voluntary work. One example is John McEwan – a long-standing member of GMB – who seems to me to symbolize much of what is wrong with employment in Britain in the 1990s. John McEwan is employed by a large chemical company on the north-west coast of England. He is also the secretary of the local social club that has over 1,200 members and a strong record of charitable work. As the club secretary, he demonstrates considerable skills as a communicator, organizer and manager; the chemical company employs him as a semi-skilled packer. The extent of John's talent came to the attention of management when the company carried out a staff aptitude and experience survey. Showing me the

results, the managing director delivered a bleak verdict, 'We are wasting the ability of about half the people who work here.'

I visit scores of workplaces each year and I believe that this enlightened manager was understating the problem. To test the issue, the GMB asked a cross-section of Union members whether they thought that their skills and talents were being properly used: 14 per cent said yes, but a massive 86 per cent said no.

Some managers comfort themselves with the notion that people prefer low-grade, undemanding work. Once again, all the evidence points the other way. Every three years, my Union commissions MORI to ask a cross-section of working people what they are seeking from work. MORI uses a prompt card suggesting a wide range of possibilities: better pay, comfortable working conditions, a manager you can respect, better holidays, a job you can be proud of and so on. Since we started the series in 1985, every poll has produced the same result: top of the list is always, 'A job which is interesting'. Interesting work always beats better pay by a wide margin; it beat job security even during the worst of the recession. The evidence suggests that interesting work is the great unsatisfied need in the British economy.

The nature of work

1996 was the centenary of William Morris' death and I re-read his book *News from Nowhere*. At university, with the practised cynicism of a 20-year-old, I dismissed the book as a piece of utopian nonsense. Thirty years later I took Morris' thesis a good deal more seriously. *News from Nowhere* gives a keen insight into the way capitalism, by emphasising the price of labour, distorts our view of the nature of work. Morris' proposition is simple and uncomfortable: every society requires certain work to be done – food has to be grown, goods have to be made and the young and old need to be cared for. Instead of regarding work as a burden to be endured for which payment has to be made, Morris reminds us that human beings actually enjoy undertaking work which is worthwhile. He suggests that a society which takes more account of human nature would see work as a boon to be shared. In his beguiling tale he goes on to demonstrate that people undertaking work as an enjoyable voluntary activity will be inclined to do it well, perhaps to a higher standard than is strictly necessary. In *News from Nowhere* work is an enriching experience for everyone, rather than a wearisome necessity which limits the enjoyment of life for a large part of the population.

The problem of pay

A trade unionist who has spent more than three decades negotiating pay rises is probably not the best person to argue that people can be happier working for nothing. Yet it is undoubtedly true, as Morris suggests, that the problem of pay gets in the way of any sensible discussion about work in our society. We cannot seem to define work with any precision. For instance, is housework really work? Not if you believe the official statistics. Is bringing up children work? Only if it is undertaken by people other than the parents. In schools, hospitals, nursing homes, in our emergency services, in the military and in many other parts of the social economy, paid and unpaid staff work alongside each other and the dividing line is certainly not drawn on the basis of relative value to clients or the community. We have reached an extraordinary state of confusion.

Sometimes conflicts arise: the paid employees worry about their job security and the volunteers worry about being taken for granted. In the search for solutions, many of us have tried to find some robust justification for the dividing line. We have all failed. Are the paid staff better qualified? Usually but not necessarily. Do the unpaid volunteers show a lower level of commitment? Most volunteers would be scandalized by the suggestion. Do the volunteers operate to lower standards? They would not be allowed to even if they wanted to. In practice, goodwill between people with common objectives helps to avoid resentment. Furthermore, of course, a vital element in creating good working relationships is the fact that the volunteers actually enjoy doing the job which they have selected.

Changing employment

Should we worry about these dilemmas? Should we try to change a society where millions of people in paid employment seem to get little satisfaction from their work and millions of people volunteer to undertake work for which they gain satisfaction but no pay? Taking even a medium-term view, I believe that we have little choice. Rapid changes in employment patterns are intensifying many of our current problems. That part of our economy where volunteering is rare – the manufacturing sector – continues to shed paid jobs. Well over three million manufacturing jobs have disappeared in the last 20 years and the trend continues. Soon only one employee in ten will work in manufacturing.

By contrast, we can forecast a rapid increase in the demand for workers in those sections of the social economy where volunteering is most strongly established. The social trend will fuel that demand. All advanced countries show an increasing demand for health and education provision. Our population is ageing and there is a rising demand for residential and nursing care. Equal career opportunities for women require that many more people work providing child care.

Most advanced countries have been very reluctant to examine the policy implications of those social trends. To be fair, the problems are formidable. Every government is wondering where it can find the money to pay the salaries of the vast number of extra people who will be needed in education, in health and in the caring professions. So it is not surprising that every government, including that of the UK, has been tempted to pretend that the gap can be filled by charities and by a substantial increase in volunteers.

The problem with this short-term expedient is that the future insists on happening. In a modern economy, the volunteer solution is really no solution at all – eventually, the bill has to be paid. If the volunteers are unemployed, we have to meet the dole payments; if the volunteers are retired, we have to meet the pensions bill; so, it is only when the volunteers are comfortably and securely employed elsewhere, or where they are supported by a well-paid partner, that no cost arises for the community. Unfortunately, our economy is rather bad at creating secure, well-paid jobs which allow sufficient leisure time for long periods of volunteering. I have heard politicians talk as if the growth of part-time work helps us towards a solution. However, in real life it is becoming more difficult for part-time workers to plan a second career as a volunteer because employers of part-time workers insist on the flexibility to change working times at short notice.

Avoiding the penalties
As the pressures increase, we might see the development of a society with nasty characteristics. The public sector pay bill may be kept down but the bill for welfare payments will go up. People who are undertaking tasks of high social value as volunteers will have to cope with the insecurity of living on state benefits. Although we will have broken the connection between pay and work the result will not be liberation but an unpleasant form of state duplicity. The Government will applaud people for undertaking voluntary work but will then begrudge them the income which they need to survive.

Anyone who believes that this forecast is too far-fetched should read the questionnaire which, since October 1996, all unemployed people have to complete when they claim the Job-Seeker's Allowance. The Government booklet makes it clear that voluntary work is officially encouraged. Indeed, volunteers are treated rather better than other claimants in respect of availability to take paid work. So far, so good. However, everyone applying for the Job-Seeker's Allowance has to answer this malicious little question: 'What is the lowest wage for which you are prepared to work?' Just in case anyone is in any doubt about the purpose of this question, the booklet explains that anyone setting a minimum pay figure which is too high runs the risk of losing their benefit. So the Government's message is: 'Keep volunteering but accept the humiliation that is appropriate for anyone who is unemployed.'

Changing the economic parameters

I believe that most people in Britain would be much happier with a different solution. We should shift that illogical and indistinct line between paid and unpaid work so that more of the work in the social economy becomes part of salaried employment. Of course, this can only be achieved if large sums of money are redistributed in our society but I believe that such an adjustment is long overdue. In essence I am proposing a new relationship between manufacturing industry and the social economy.

Fifty years ago a good part of the wealth created by manufacturing industry was spread throughout the population because manufacturing industry employed and paid wages to so many people. Manufacturing industry provided goods and provided the incomes that allowed those goods to be purchased. Just as important, the manufacturing sector provided the taxes which paid for the welfare state and the rest of the infrastructure of a civilized society. Not any more. In the modern world, as I have shown, manufacturing industry may still be a wonderful engine for creating wealth but it does not create jobs. Moreover, the tax burden on British industry has also been substantially reduced: it is now the lowest in Europe and one of the lowest anywhere in the world – unless an adjustment is made, Britain will never be able to pay for the education, health, caring and social services that we all require for a civilized life.

The solution will certainly involve higher taxation of manufacturing interests. However, other countries have combined higher taxation with more imaginative schemes, whereby manufacturing companies sponsor or pay directly for social projects. Yet no matter how sensitively it is done, the companies concerned will not like it. They will protest that they are part of a global economy and that extra social costs will reduce competitiveness. Fortunately, the counter argument is strong. Competitiveness depends on investment in people and technology, and British manufacturing industry as a whole is rather bad at both. By international standards, a high proportion of the wealth of British manufacturing industry goes into dividend payments to shareholders. There is plenty of room in the British economy for wealth-creating investment, as well as for the transfer of resources to satisfy the social needs of an advanced country.

Taking opportunities

In conclusion, I return to the wider challenge with which I began. Can we use these difficult and controversial changes to create employment which is more interesting and more satisfying for most of our people? The opportunities are considerable. Much employment in the social economy is intrinsically worthwhile because the jobs are focused on meeting obvious human needs. With the extra advantage of new technology, there is little doubt that we have the capacity to design jobs which are self-evidently valuable and satisfying: jobs which attract volunteers because they are jobs to be proud of.

We would be more certain of success if we decided to apply a little more of William Morris' liberating ideology: people work best when they make their own decisions about how work should be done. For nearly two centuries, most of the jobs in Britain have been organized by managers to fit particular production processes. The constraints that now exist come not from the demands of technology but from the way we are conditioned to expect decisions to be made by the people at the top. People are reservoirs of untapped talent and there is no good reason why workers should not now take the prime responsibility for designing their own jobs.

In simple terms, our aim should be to create jobs fit for volunteers but with the security of a decent salary. We should take the opportunity provided by rapid changes in employment both to redefine and to redesign what we mean by work. If we are successful we can coin a new term to describe the nature of work in Britain. We should wave goodbye to the era of the wage slave and joyfully enter the period when we can refer to the workforce of Britain as 'paid volunteers'.

THE BROMLEY BY BOW CENTRE – A MODEL FOR COMMUNITY DEVELOPMENT

The Francis C. Scott Memorial Lecture

REVEREND ANDREW MAWSON

Chairman, Bromley by Bow Centre
Executive Director, Community Action Network (CAN)

Four miles east of the City of London sits Bromley by Bow, an ancient community mentioned by Chaucer, once at the heart of the Industrial Revolution but now a forgotten corner at the extreme eastern edge of the London Borough of Tower Hamlets. The 1991 Department of the Environment Index of Local Conditions ranked Tower Hamlets first in intensity of deprivation and second in extent of any local authority in the country. Bromley Ward has the second highest indices of deprivation in East London (19.06 against an East London average of 9.78) but has had little investment – some derelict sites date back to the Second World War – being situated outside the scope of various government initiatives, such as City Challenge.

The area demonstrates many of the worst aspects of urban decay: poor health (16.3 per cent of residents have long-term illness); poor housing (more than 90 per cent is rented); and poor educational achievement (only 18 per cent get 4 GCSEs or above). It is an area of high population density, high levels of unemployment (males 31.5

per cent, ethnic minorities 47.3 per cent) and a diverse ethnic minority population (36 per cent ethnic minorities). Bordered by two major highways, it is disconnected from adjacent areas, which contributes to problems of isolation and the need for a community focus.

Despite these difficulties Bromley by Bow houses a wealth of talent and opportunities, in part due to its extraordinary diversity. This potential, however, is not being released. The City, with its wealth and influence, is on our doorstep. It is just now that it is beginning to realize the role it can play in unlocking the potential here and the benefits to be gained by engaging with the creativity and enterprise of its neighbours.

The Bromley by Bow Centre
The Bromley by Bow Centre began in 1983 when the small, elderly church congregation offered their underused buildings to the community. A number of artists living in the area became involved, giving classes to local people in return for rent-free workshop space. Others followed their example and a nursery, cafe, dance school and disability groups were set up, benefiting both individuals and the wider community.

Since then we have sought to create a community space in which the entrepreneurial potential and creativity of local people can be explored. Projects have evolved around five pillars: health, education, the arts, environment and enterprise. The Centre has grown to include community care services, community education activities, art projects, ethnic minority programmes, health projects and urban regeneration schemes. Phase 1 of the redevelopment of a derelict park site adjacent to our buildings has now been completed and a £1.5 million initiative to build a new GP and Primary Care Centre was finished in May 1997. This is the first integrated community health facility of its kind in the country with the unique distinction of being owned directly by local people, with GPs paying rent to patients.

The church at the Bromley by Bow Centre stands at the heart of the project both physically and psychologically. The liturgical space has been redesigned and remains a core sanctuary around which the bustle of the day revolves. Like the medieval cathedral, the church sits amidst the marketplace of everyday activity, allowing the vibrancy and diversity of life to surround it and enabling a mutual crossover of influence between the secular and sacred.

Traditional models of community development have generally failed the inner city – and the church, either working in isolation from the rest of the world or hand in glove with the structures, has failed to be the carrier of effective transformation. Our aim is to create effective social change within a framework of local, private and public sector partnership, leading to a community of confident individuals who are in a position to engage with the issues and bring about their own transformations. It is therefore a model which is constantly changing.

People not structures
The Bromley by Bow Centre has grown around the energy of individuals rather than structures or systems. This is a community marked by a huge social deficit and key staff are charged with the task of being entrepreneurial in their work: creating social capital amongst the groups they work with. In this respect they are employed not to manage projects but to create environments which encourage a sense of vision and motivation.

People themselves are the bricks of any sustainable regeneration process and community growth is dependent upon creating opportunities for individual growth. It is a process dependent on the personal relationships which have grown between staff and local people over a number of years, partnerships based on mutuality and friendship. We have dispensed with sentimentality about the nature of democracy and the need for everyone to be involved in every decision, consciously avoided consultation, meetings and forums as these structures are familiar tools and disempower local people further. The majority of people in this community do not run their lives around pieces of paper but are more likely to communicate through conversations and engaging in each other's lives. It is therefore at this point that our process of consultation begins.

New frameworks for operation

The need to create structures which recognize the complexities of people's lives led us to encourage a loose–tight framework of operation: loose enough to allow people the freedom either to be proactive or to respond quickly to ideas but tight enough to offer a framework of values which contribute to an overall sense of direction.

Our organizational structures do not define what is acceptable or unacceptable. The reality of people's lives on our estates is too complex to legislate around ideology or policies and so, for instance, we do not exclude people from the project for racism or sexism. There is recognition that the language of the street does not always have the abusive meaning interpreted by the politically correct and even when it is abusive, the context is generally too complicated to be resolved simply by a policy of exclusion. We have found that excluding people or views simply denies the complexities of the issues. It leads to an unhealthy environment in which everyone has the same views and in which the tensions arising from our diversity are lost as creative opportunities. Moving forward is dependent on making the connections between people not severing the links.

The reality of life in the inner city is one of messiness. A sense of insecurity and the inability to plan or commit to anything regular is a prevalent pattern of existence for many people. We have therefore tried to create points of rhythm and regularity to the week, for example the Sunday liturgy, community cafe or gardening projects around which people can focus their lives.

Similarly, the only way to enable people to participate in wider opportunities is to be flexible in the provision of services. To ensure courses are accessible to those who most need them, we have structured our NVQ (National Vocational Qualification) Care training courses around people's lives rather than around our organizational needs. Ironically, this has prevented us from accessing the usual sources of training funding because it is impossible to achieve strict output measures. This approach calls into question the structures set up to support community-based training, for instance via Training and Enterprise Councils, and has forced us to find alternative methods of evaluating the impact of community development programmes.

Integration not compartmentalization
In an increasingly fragmented world agents of change must bring people together, for the energy for real change lies in the creativity of these connections. Our experience of dealing with public finances, with five or six different government departments all at the same time, has demonstrated the wastage of limited public funds when human beings are dealt with in a disconnected way – education, health, housing and employment and so on.

Within the present building, spaces are claimed by specific groups such as the nursery or artists, and are managed in a way that encourages a sense of ownership but without privatization. The spaces are designed to be used by different groups simultaneously and solutions have to be found which suit everyone. The need to share resources means people have to rub shoulders with those they might otherwise prefer to ignore and the possibilities for integration begin. This allows the inevitable tension which arises from our diversity to become an opportunity for dialogue rather than a block to communication.

There are few spaces in our society where people from across the spectrum of life meet and connect – the general pattern is one of compartmentalization. It is rare for the different disciplines, never mind ideologies, of art, health, education, the environment and enterprise to be so intrinsically linked. We have found, however, that it is only by creating a wide range of partnerships and pushing the process of integration deeper into our frameworks that regeneration initiatives, equal to the complexities of the issues, can be found.

The designed environment as a means of change
The places in which we live and work have a profound effect upon the way we feel about ourselves; the designed environment is not only a physical statement of who we are but also of how we are valued. At Bromley by Bow the physical and emotional environment of the Centre is designed to reflect the high value we place upon people who use it. The buildings have become a statement of our commitment to creating environments based on integration, creativity and excellence.

Quality and excellence are important when designing project environments. The buildings are designed and furnished to a high standard using wood and quality materials and the project is surrounded with works of art to instil a sense of beauty and inspiration. This is in stark contrast to the cheap, degenerate environment of the surrounding area which reinforces the sense of failure which has undermined this community for decades.

Our aim is to lift the low self-esteem of individuals by creating opportunities for excellence and achievement and to open up the world of possibilities by encouraging people to dream. Everyone has something to contribute to community life and the simple act of expecting people to achieve rather than fail has enabled dreams to become reality. Many people in the inner city have been damaged by decades of inadequate resourcing and their dreams reflect this low sense of expectation.

Instead of asking people what they would like to do, we present opportunities which have the effect of opening up new experiences: going to the Sinai Desert, an art gallery, the Ritz for afternoon tea. An important part of this process is to offer enough support to make the impossible become a reality and it is here that the arts have a critical role to play.

New community values and ideas

New ideas and values come through the interaction of unlikely partners. Recently a partnership has been brought together in Bromley by Bow to design and build a new children's play area in a three-acre park. A local group of young people are working to design a play area with scientists from the Department of Haematology at Great Ormond Street Children's Hospital, scientists and engineers from Aldermaston Nuclear Weapons Site and artists from the Bromley by Bow Centre. The project, entitled The Rivers Within, has been sponsored by COPUS, a body concerned with the public understanding of science. When the project is completed we will build a play space which, in an amusing way, practically illustrates the biological workings of the human body. The play equipment might include a DNA dragon, teeth stepping stones, a bouncing tummy and a brain maze.

This initiative is a practical opportunity for scientists, artists and children – the next generation – to explore each other's worlds, disciplines, values and ideas and to work together on a practical task.

A HOME FOR LIFE
AND LIVING FOR THE
TWENTY-FIRST CENTURY

MICHAEL HOLYER

Chairman, Habinteg Housing Association

The title of this sounds somewhat futuristic, but in terms of design and building, decisions have to be taken now – or should already have been taken – to produce homes for the twenty-first century. Much development is required before 'Smart homes' (see pages 97–98) and the like can be considered as practical propositions for general housing applications, so I am going to discuss innovation that is under way now.

To use the title of a book by Arundhati Roy which found fame in 1997 by collecting the Booker Prize, I am going to consider a matter which could be the province of 'the God of Small Things', for it is the small things that make a difference to living, that are achievable now, and that can be taken into the next century. I shall therefore introduce the concept of Lifetime Homes, an adaptable and flexible approach to the design of our future homes. I shall use a fable format to explain the basic ideas of Lifetime Homes, for it allows a certain amount of artistic licence, while permitting the inclusion of pertinent points from which a moral can be drawn.

The fable of Jack and Jill
Imagine twins being born, a boy and a girl, called Jack and Jill. Jack was the first to enter the world in a rapid delivery: Jill followed a long while after, and due to complications, suffered damage which

resulted in some impairment of the use of her limbs. As the children grew, it was apparent that both had average ability in educational terms but at the time they went to school, special units existed and, because of her physical disability, Jill was put into one such unit. Not unnaturally she resented this because of the degree of exclusion which resulted from such an arrangement.

Both Jack and Jill at the end of their schooling achieved reasonable O and A level results (it was before the time of GCSEs). Jack decided to go on to university but, because of her experiences at school, and not wishing to leave herself open to more isolation at university, Jill decided to take an Open University course.

Both twins successfully completed degree courses and both thereafter married. Jill and her husband lived in a flat and, fortunately, he was reasonably skilled in DIY, so was able to build in some basic adaptations, which made Jill's life a little easier, until the day they decided that they wanted a family and realized that, for Jill to cope with a house and a baby, rather more suitable accommodation would have to be found.

They approached the Local Authority and had their names put onto the housing list, at the appropriate time enquiring if the necessary accommodation could be provided. The authority advised them that, while they had no suitable accommodation currently available, a local Housing Association had just finished a development, which could possibly offer them what they wanted. The housing officer of this association suggested they visit the development to check whether it met their needs. When they arrived at the scheme, Jill was rather disappointed, as it looked like any other housing estate and seemed to have nothing special to offer. They were invited to tour a house by themselves initially, as the housing officer said he had some pressing business to attend to but would return shortly. Jill, who was by this time fairly heavily pregnant and temporarily confined to a wheelchair, and her husband toured the house and were, again, rather disappointed, as there appeared to be nothing particularly special about the property, except that there was no step to negotiate at either the front or back door and it was reasonably easy to get around on the ground floor.

The Housing Officer returned, apologized for his absence, and enquired what they thought of the house. When Jill said that it looked like any other house, she was surprised to see a broad grin appear on the housing officer's face. He told Jill and her husband that this was a Lifetime Home, as were all the other houses on the estate and, while not specifically designed for people in wheelchairs, it could be adapted if required to suit various circumstances, with reasonable ease and cost.

He said that the whole estate was built on the basis that all dwellings were accessible to everyone which, he explained, readily allowed visits to and from neighbours, as there were no physical barriers to prevent this. He took them outside and showed them that the estate had been laid out with minimal gradients, dropped kerbs and level access, which allowed a person in a wheelchair or a mother pushing say a twin pushchair to do so with ease.

THE 16 LIFETIME HOMES STANDARDS
The housing officer then took Jill and her husband around the property, pointing out the 16 standards which go to make up the Lifetime Homes concept:

1 The parking space was close to the entrance of the house, with a gentle slope to the entrance porch.

2 The parking space made provision for widening up to 3.3 metres.

3 If necessary it could be covered, to allow dry transfer from car to porch.

4 At the entrance there was an illuminated canopy so that, when you are fumbling for keys in the rain, with perhaps poor eyesight, you, your child and your shopping remain dry. The porch floor was level, making it easy to move from outside to inside. (Jill asked if the rain didn't get in under the door: the Housing Officer assured her that many

installations had been built, using one of the details shown in the illustration and that none, to date, had leaked.)

5 Sixteen flats on the estate had lift access and were all wheelchair accessible by reason of the level lift access, door width, car size and control locations.

6 The width of all doorways, hallways and corridors were built to slightly wider dimensions than normal.

7 There was sufficient space included in the design of kitchens, dining areas and sitting rooms, and adequate circulation space for wheelchair users everywhere.

8 The sitting room or family room was at entrance level for ease of access for visitors and disabled family members.

9 In the houses, there was space on the ground floor that can be used as a convenient bed space. Equipment could provide access to upstairs for older and disabled people.

10 There was a downstairs toilet which was wheelchair accessible, with drainage and service provision, so a shower could be fitted at any time.

11 Walls to the bathroom and toilet were built to allow for adaptations, such as handrails.

12 The design of the stair incorporated provision for a future stair lift. Some houses had a landing incorporated halfway up the stairs as a pausing place to assist the elderly.

13 The bathroom and bedroom ceilings were constructed to be strong enough, or capable of being made strong enough, to support a hoist at a later date. Within the wall between the bedroom and adjacent bathroom, provision was made for the installation of a future floor to ceiling door to connect the two rooms by a hoist.

14 The bathroom layout was designed to incorporate ease of access to the bath and toilet, and the washbasin was also accessible. There is a shelf at the end of the bath, to sit on and swing your legs over.

15   The officer explained that the living room window glazing was less than 800 millimetres above the floor level, allowing older and disabled people who need to feel in touch with the outside world, a clear view when seated. He also showed that all windows were easy to open and operate, while at the same time containing child safety devices.

16   Switches, sockets and service controls were all located at heights between 600 and 1200 millimetres above the floor, thus producing a zone accessible to young, old and disabled or non-disabled.

The housing officer also pointed out that in this house an area had been identified, and construction provided, for the possible installation of a house lift running between the living room and main bedroom, with adjacent bathroom. He said this allowance was made to accommodate a wheelchair user who wished to sleep at first floor level, while living at ground floor level. Jill said she supposed that people like her may eventually wish to have such an installation but couldn't understand what happened to the hole in the first floor. The officer explained that, when the lift platform was at ground level, a high level infill panel filled the first floor hole and when the lift was at first floor level, the underside of the lift platform was finished to match the ceiling.

Jill's husband said he could understand these controlling dimensions were necessary for wheelchair users but questioned the need for them generally. It was explained to him that the house may be occupied by elderly people, who would find it difficult to bend down to use sockets at the normal low level, or reach up to switches at a high level, and this was the reason for this dimensional zone.

After all this detail, Jill's husband was happy that this was the house for them but Jill still had one area of concern. She explained that she was in a wheelchair at present because of her pregnancy, but would probably be able to dispense with this some time after the birth, so she was worried the two possible worktop height requirements for the kitchen. The officer said that, due to his association's long experience with similar problems, in wheelchair units, kitchen fittings could be provided which allowed an adjustment of the worktop height and included flexible and adjustable service and wastes. He said that the variable worktop height would not be a problem, and, because all the special provisions made to adapt the house had been considered at the outset, height adaptations required could be accommodated with the minimum of inconvenience and cost.

Jill and her husband moved into the house on the new estate and had two children. Jill no longer felt isolated, as she was able to easily visit neighbours. There were, however, problems when she visited Jack and his family, as there were steps up to the front door and she found, as time went by, that she could no longer get into his house without help, as she was back in her wheelchair. She also found that once inside Jack's home she was unable to move around the ground floor easily, due to the design of the corridors and doors, and it was impossible to use the ground floor toilet.

She eventually had to stop visiting, so Jack had to visit her. Meanwhile, he had stopped playing sport some years before and found that in his 50s he needed to have a hip replacement and knee joint operation, due to too much football. Both Jack and Jill's children had all left home and Jack thought as he aged, things might get worse. Being very conversant with his sister's house and the provision that it had, which allowed her to operate with reasonable freedom, he called in a local builder with a view to having some adaptations made to his house to make life easier in the future.

The builder, as some builders do, listened to the alterations Jack wanted and shook his head from side to side, saying that all was possible but that it would be very expensive. Jack decided to get a second opinion and received a similar response but that builder asked if Jack had noticed a new building that was going up just along the road, which he was constructing. As the speculative building market was becoming very competitive, he had thought he would steal a march on his rivals by adopting many of the Lifetime

Home criteria, which gave him a sales advantage at very little extra cost.

Jack looked at the house and decided that, while he would probably not require all the adaptations at present, and possibly some never, it would be sensible to make the move before he was forced to. He and Jill were able to visit one another again, so those who were united in the womb were reunited in life.

Provisions today: a home for tomorrow

Partially retired myself, I am becoming conscious of the ageing process. Research has shown that the UK has a population that lives longer and longer. We are likely to follow America in that our predicted lifespan of about 85 years will probably extend by another 15 years and will naturally bring about problems which the present housing stock, social and house services, will be hard-pressed to address.

Huge savings in expenditure could be made by the ease of adapting a house that already has provision for adaptations to be built in. There would be dramatic savings to health and care services if people could remain independently, or with some support, in their own homes for longer.

The moral of the fable is to recognize that, by making fairly minimal provisions today, which are economical and politically expedient, 'the God of Small Things' can provide a Home for Life and Living for the Twenty-First Century.

THE INCLUSIVE HOMES OF THE FUTURE

RICHARD BEST

Director, Joseph Rowntree Foundation

Instead of shutting people out – or evicting or imprisoning those who move into houses and face temporary or permanent disabilities later – tomorrow's homes will be far more inclusive. As Michael Holyer has demonstrated (pages 89–95), Lifetime Homes are not a pipedream. The pioneering work of the Habinteg Housing Association and the Joseph Rowntree Foundation, with valuable support from national organizations such as RADAR (the Royal Association for Disability and Rehabilitation), the Access Committee for England, Age Concern and others, has led to the Government amending an extension to Part M of the Building Regulations: the new regulations, effective from autumn 1999, put the UK up with the leading nations in making all new homes more accessible.

Smart homes
Technological advances devised first for people with disabilities can often become the norm for everyone else. We now take it for granted that new cars will have 'smart' features such as central locking and electric windows – concepts originally intended to benefit those who found it awkward to handle these tasks without assistance. The Joseph Rowntree Foundation is currently working on the creation of Smart Homes: the innovations have been devised for the convenience of older or disabled occupiers

but everyone will want the new technology when they see it in action.

Working in co-operation with Edinvar Housing Association in Scotland, we are at an advanced stage in using the kind of sensors now familiar in security systems, and the hand-held remote controls which we all use to operate our televisions and videos, to perform new functions in the home. We can now send messages down the mains wiring, activated by an infra-red receiver mounted in a ceiling rose: we can draw the curtains, open the windows, turn on table lamps, lock any door in the house. A gas detector not only sounds the alarm, it also turns off the gas, alerts a central call station and opens the window. When the doorbell goes, the little video camera beams a picture to the television set and announces that there is 'someone at the door'. By pressing the appropriate icon on the hand-held control, a range of commands can be set, for example we can fill the bath to exactly half full at a predetermined temperature. We also have a system, particularly for people suffering from dementia, by which sensors can beam a series of messages to a resident warden.

Other features of future housing
It seems likely that tomorrow's new homes will also incorporate flexible design which, for example, will allow internal walls to be moved around – as is common in the Netherlands – or roof space to be speedily converted to meet changed circumstances. At the same time environmental concerns will lead increasingly to use of sustainable building materials and to new energy-saving and water conservation features (see pages 107–121).

Foreign competition?
It is an open question whether the UK's construction industry, as currently constituted, will lead the way in implementing innovative concepts. The industry is notorious for its underfunding of training and, mostly because it must play safe in catering for the most conservative tastes in the market, it lacks innovation. We persist, for

example, with antiquated building methods on site, where other countries – particularly Japan and the Netherlands – have perfected precision building of the component parts in factory conditions. Are we going to need to import overseas builders to stimulate change here – just as other industries have been forced to modernize by foreign competition?

Building more
As well as building better, like it or not we must build more.

FIVE MILLION HOMES
Everyone has become familiar with the statistic of 4.4 million extra households who will need homes in the future. There are some important points to make about this:

- The 4.4 million extra households represents the growth, based on past trends, for the 25 years from 1991 to 2016. This implies lower levels of growth in the 1990s than in the 1980s, with further falls for subsequent decades – so the figures are not particularly sensational.

- But numbers of households do not represent the whole story. As well as finding somewhere for the new households to go we must replace any properties that are demolished. Annual levels of demolition have fallen from some 80,000 in the 1970s to just 5,000 in the mid 1990s. At this rate, every new home built today would have to stand for 5,600 years before being replaced! It seems certain that some of the older property – including some of the worst designed and built council estates of the 1960s and 1970s – will have to come down over the decades ahead. Thus replacements (after deducting gains from conversions of existing properties) will add to requirements for new homes.

- It is important to make some inroads into the backlog of currently unmet need. The brilliant statistical work we commissioned from Alan Holmans – previously chief housing economist at the Department of the Environment – showed that over 500,000 households at the beginning of the period were overcrowded, living in bed and breakfast hotels or hostels, or even on the streets. If, by 2016, the position is to be improved, not just held at today's levels, some of this unmet need must be met.

- In terms of the number of homes to be built, therefore, rather than the number of households which will be formed, our estimate is for a total of more than 5 million over the 25-year term.

But why will so many more households be formed when the birth rate is relatively static? There are three main reasons for this:

- First, it is not the number of babies but the number of adults that counts in the creation of new, independent households. With the 'baby boomers' forming homes as adults, there is substantial growth coming through the pipeline. When coupled with the net gain from immigration – now almost entirely from Europe, rather than from the old Commonwealth and now estimated as contributing an extra 20,000 households a year – 46 per cent of the growth comprises more, new, adult households.

- Second, our changed behaviour – with more of us never marrying and more of us divorcing and separating – will greatly enhance the number of households with one person not two or more. This factor accounts for 33 per cent of overall growth in households. We may wish that the next generation will marry and stay together for life, but substantial changes in current patterns of behaviour cannot be expected in the next few years.

- Third, our longer lives mean we go on occupying the same homes, when previously these would have been vacated for the next generation; in these circumstances, too, the home will often be occupied by just one person.

Eighty per cent of the extra households will comprise people living on their own, but the growth is not amongst youngsters leaving home for university or job reasons (since that bulge has mostly occurred already); rather it is amongst those from their late twenties through to old age. It does not follow that building for the next century will mean small flats and shared accommodation: most of those in the growth categories will have the personal resources to pay their own way – buying or renting in the market – and are unlikely to choose hostels or shared accommodation. Failing to build enough self-contained homes for all will not squeeze middle-aged single people into shared flats since these people will have the money to do as they please. It is new, poorer households – the group least able to compete in the marketplace – who will suffer if we do not have enough housing for everyone.

A member of the House of Commons Environment Committee suggested that people would change their behaviour if they knew there were fewer homes being built: reduce supply and you will reduce demand. But history shows that people grow up, create families, or divorce/separate, or, indeed, live longer, irrespective of the housing market. Household formation reached its peak after the Second World War following a period in which no homes had been built for many years and there had been extensive demolition by bombing. The analogy with road building – that if fewer roads are built, there will be fewer cars on the roads – does not work at all for housing.

'Greenfield' land
Why cannot most of these new homes be built on 'brownfield land' in urban areas, not on the greenfields of rural England?

Professor Tony Champion of Newcastle University has tracked the 'cascade' of population away from London and the major conurbations, with the greatest growth emerging in the most remote rural areas. Even though the proportion of land occupied by housing will only rise by 1.3 per cent – from 10.6 per cent to 11.9 per cent – over the 25 years to 2016 if current trends continue, few would deny the environmental importance in achieving as much new building as possible within our towns and cities.

Many of the best urban sites, however, have been developed. Indeed, 12 per cent of recent urban development has been on playing fields and open spaces in our towns: cramming more houses onto the green sites will only hasten the urban exodus by reducing the quality of life in towns and cities. Many of the remaining sites cannot be developed without extensive decontamination and environmental improvements – for which we taxpayers may be unwilling to pay. (The polluters are usually long gone.)

Most new homes are built by private housebuilders and however many acres of derelict brownfield land you can show them – whether in dejected post-industrial northern cities or on the extremities of East London – these developers will sit on their hands and do nothing rather than construct new housing which would stand empty and unsold.

Blanket prohibitions on new housing will not lead to developments on brownfield, inner city sites. (Anyway, half of all the homes in the Shire counties are needed for people already living there.) The key to more urban building lies in planning policies, public attitudes and government investment in urban areas.

Urban regeneration
Even though the job market has changed dramatically, the metropolitan areas can re-invent themselves as centres of learning, of services, of new industries, of leisure and entertainment.

Changing the image, and the attractiveness, of city living is not just about housing: it is about improving safety, schools, parks, air quality, transport, amenities and facilities. In short, it is about taking an holistic approach to the renewal of urban life. I have joined with others in asking Government for an Urban White Paper to take this approach forward across all government Departments and am delighted that one is to be published.

Social housing
Of course housing is critical to this process of 'urban renaissance'. 'Social housing' – subsidized housing for those who cannot afford what they need – which is required for more than a third of tomorrow's new households, is an essential component. Even though Government is to allow local authorities to spend the unspent, accumulated receipts from sales of council housing under the Right to Buy policy – estimated at about £5 billion – total resources available for social housebuilding will remain near all-time low levels in the next few years. And worries about inadequate numbers of such homes are not the only concern: there are fears, too, about where social housing will go. If it is used to fill those brownfield sites in the areas where people who can exercise choice will not go, then the stigma and the segregation attaching to social housing will grow worse; and by concentrating all those on the very lowest incomes in the inner city, the flight of the economically independent – just as in the big cities of the United States – will be accelerated.

Creating strong communities
Following the tenets of Joseph Rowntree, my organization has attempted – for nearly 100 years – to create strong communities when building new homes. Recognizing that a new estate of social housing which is exclusively for rent and exclusively for those in the very greatest need is inimical to forming a strong new community, we have built three developments in the 1990s - with an average of 125 Lifetime Homes each – on the basis of Mixed and Flexible Tenure. Under this arrangement, home owners are scattered amongst the rented housing, in identical homes, thereby breaking

down barriers between tenures and the segregation of poor households. Our aim is to ensure there are role models of people going out to work, for the children on the estate; and that there are residents of different income levels providing some mix and balance. All our tenants have the opportunity to purchase shares in the ownership of their home, up to full ownership; and those who buy have the chance to sell shares back to us – becoming tenants if need be – if they get into serious financial difficulty. Coupled with policies for involving residents in decisions about their homes we believe this model of social housing can help combat the growth of social exclusion, of groups cut off from the opportunities and aspirations in the rest of society.

City-centre apartments for single people

But estates of social housing – however sensitively developed and managed – will not revive our cities. We need the inward movement of those with decent incomes, skills and leadership qualities, who have been moving out and commuting in for work or leisure. It is unrealistic to expect families with young children to flock back to the city centres until the bigger problems of crime, education and health are the subject of concerted effort. But we can make a start with some of those middle-income single people who represent such a significant proportion of household growth.

The Rowntree Foundation has started building the first of two new developments of City-centre Apartments for Single People at Affordable Rents – CASPAR projects. Our aim is to demonstrate to other investors – since we are substantial investors ourselves – that it makes good sense to put money into rented accommodation which is purpose-built for single people and childless couples. If we succeed, we will save greenfield sites elsewhere by developing unused urban land, cut down on the congestion and pollution of commuter traffic and help to revive our inner city areas.

Our first development is in Birmingham and we plan to start the second shortly in Leeds. If the idea catches on, investment would flow into other conurbations up and down the country and a market would emerge of a kind entirely familiar in the rest of Europe and North America. Without the need to appease the home buyer, these rented homes can be designed and built in more innovative ways.

Retirement communities
Meanwhile, to the north of York, we have just finished building a Continuing Care Retirement Community, modelled on similar projects pioneered by the Quakers in the United States. These comprise high quality bungalows surrounding a centre for leisure – with a gym, spa pool and restaurant – and both full residential nursing facilities and care services which can be delivered to your bungalow. Two hundred and fifty people are moving into this pioneering development, which aims to provide financial security by requiring everyone to pay an annual service charge that remains constant whatever care needs may emerge in the future. By pooling the fixed charge – around £4,500 per annum – we can cover all the costs of high quality, long-term care for the minority who will need it.

We see the Retirement Communities of this kind as an antidote to loneliness and physical insecurity, offering the chance to lead a more fulfilling life through a range of facilities and amenities, to provide a stimulating retirement. Of course, the pattern will not suit everyone: but we have already sold all of the places in this first development and have a waiting list.

Continuing Care Retirement Communities (CCRCs) have obvious environmental benefits too: they can be relatively high density, with less need to pay attention to car parking; and most of those moving in are likely to free up a much larger family home elsewhere. Thus these new communities can help us disproportionately to meet the challenges of those five million extra homes.

In conclusion

Some of these inclusive housing measures require huge effort at the highest level – devising and implementing a truly holistic strategy for our urban areas – and some pick-up on the small things, such as the height of power points or the gas detector which opens the window. But the measures advocated by the Rowntree Foundation, and by other organizations such as Habinteg Housing Association, Anchor and the Peabody Trust, all aim to ensure that living in the twenty-first century means fewer people being excluded as they are now, either by the houses themselves or by the ways we have been segregating and stigmatizing the poorer, while encouraging those who are economically independent to move outwards from our cities and towns. The aim is both better lives for us individually and stronger communities where we can live more harmoniously together.

GREENING THE BUILDING AND THE BOTTOM LINE

AMORY B. LOVINS

Director of Research,
Rocky Mountain Institute, Inc.,
Snowmass, Colorado, USA

I shall be exploring green architecture: the way to create serene and beautiful structures that grow organically in and from their place – structures that don't exploit or pollute but rather increase harmony with the whole world round them. Too much modern building design is not like that at all. Perhaps a society can get too good at technical artifice and can be tempted to do things because they're do-able, not because they are a good idea.

Too many modern commercial buildings wall people off from the outdoors, and immerse them in conditioned air and artificial light, cocooning them in uniform banality. The air in such buildings comes from coils and fans rather than from trees and gardens. The light comes from phosphors, not our neighbourhood star. The sounds come from humming motors and lighting ballasts, from centrifugal fans and duct resonances, rather than from songbirds and waterfalls. The diversions come from acrid fumes and eye-hurting glare rather than from flowers and butterflies and the scent of jasmine.

However skilful the designers, buildings conceived in that spirit cannot provide the conditions in which people evolved, in which the body is healthy and alert, the spirit tranquil and nourished. But so pervasive has this travesty of architecture become that very few people today have ever experienced real comfort in a building – thermal, visual or acoustic comfort – so they hardly know what they are missing.

Understanding physical needs

To provide such comfort we first need to understand what the body wants. A lot of ideas about this come from the East, particularly from Japan, where they have an idea utterly contrary to the comfort theory used by building services engineers in the West (although it is an obvious one to any evolutionary biologist). It is the notion that people will prefer and will thrive in a subtly dynamic environment rather than a static one. Modern Japanese air-conditioners in rooms slightly vary the temperature, using a pseudo-random number generator, and deliver air not in a steady flow but in a series of pseudo-random gusts that imitate natural breezes. Air-handling systems in large Japanese buildings might occasionally add subliminal traces of fragrance, perhaps a whiff of sandalwood, to stimulate the sensorium. This approach to air-conditioning is in the same spirit in which Japanese tea-cups are beautiful to hold and Japanese food beautiful to see: one of the great contributions of that culture is the notion that technology is first of all an art form to be judged on aesthetic criteria.

By contrast, a typical Western building services engineer will strive to eliminate every such pesky trace of variability, with thermostats and humidistats and photosensors, so that the human experience is rendered uniform and constant down to the last lux of light and molecule of air, as if people were dead machines rather than dynamic organisms. All too often the architect – some of whom seem to have forgotten where the sun is – will design a box that is randomly oriented, of the all-glass-and-no-windows variety, shuttered with blinds and curtains to block any natural light that might somehow find its way in. Disagreeable draughts of cold and hot air are then noisily blown at people to try to overcome the airlessness, chill, or heat of the poorly conceived building envelope.

Controlled ventilation replaces operable windows, and glaring downlights embedded in dark ceilings replace the luminous sky under which people first evolved. In every case the artificial substitutes for the natural conditions are less and worse. They don't let people do or be or feel their best.

Designing greener buildings
Mindful of these needs, many design professionals are now evolving an art and science of green design that can create magical buildings, and some of those buildings already exist. You know when you are in one because it combines superior human and financial performance. (This combination is documented in over 100 case studies in Rocky Mountain Institute's book *Green Development: Integrating Ecology and Real Estate*[1] and CD-ROM *Green Developments.*[2]) It creates delight when entered, harmony when occupied and regret when departed.

Green buildings can be built in practically any desired style or size, programme or climate. They simply – or at least it seems simple when it's all done – combine a biologically and spiritually informed appreciation of what people are and want, a completely integrated design process and a toolkit of advanced technologies. They require design to yield a result that is simple, not complex; passive, not active; gracefully responsive rather than stubbornly resistant to climate, sunlight and weather; and uniquely optimized, not formulaic.

Making big resource savings costs less than small ones
From economic theory, we are used to supposing that the more energy or resources we save, the more and more steeply the cost of saving the next unit rises, until we hit the limit of cost-effectiveness and stop. That is indeed often true up to a point, but what is often overlooked is that in many instances, if we keep going and save some more, we can often tunnel through a cost barrier to the point where the cost comes down again and we end up with bigger savings and lower costs.

The Rocky Mountain Institute building

The Rocky Mountain Institute building in western Colorado at an elevation of 7,100 feet (2,164 metres) is an example of how well green architecture can work and how cost-effective such buildings can be. It is a rather odd-looking building – though it needn't be – that combines a house, indoor banana farm and research centre in a total of about 4,000 square feet (372 square metres). It is subjected to quite a severe climate with lowest temperatures of about −44°C. The growing season between hard frosts is from about 26 June to 16 August, but there might be a frost on any day of the year, so it is like having two seasons, winter and July. It is not reliably sunny, and we have had on occasion 39 days of continuous cloud in mid-winter.

Nonetheless, you can come into the atrium of the building out of a blizzard and find yourself in a jungle of banana trees, avocados, mangos, guavas, loquats, passion fruit, papaya, grapes, bougainvillea and so on. You come in to the odour of night-blooming jasmine, the song of frogs, the sound of the Japanese waterfall tuned to alpha rhythm and the sight of lizards, a pygmy hedgehog, and insects used (instead of pesticides) for controlling pests.

Heating and insulation

Then you realize there is no heating system other than two small wood-stoves – we have to burn the energy studies somehow – and passive solar heating. This is because of super-insulation. The walls are about twice and the ceiling three times as well insulated as what would normally be considered optimal. We recover about 92 per cent of the ventilation heat through air-to-air heat exchangers.

The key to the whole design is superwindows. They are ordinary-looking windows incorporating two or three special films that transmit light very well but reflect infra-red. They are filled with a heavy gas like argon or krypton so they insulate as well as six, nine or even twelve sheets of glass. Even the original 1983 units, which were only as good as six sheets of glass, gained more heat than they lost, facing in any direction including north, because the diffuse skylight plus the snow bounce brings in more energy than you lose. Our task is simply to balance that heat gain against the heat losses, down to the last per cent or so.

CONSTRUCTION AND COSTS

Money was saved in construction because we eliminated the heating system, reducing capital cost by more than the heat-trapping technologies increased it. We put that saved money towards making other savings. Ninety-nine per cent of water-heating energy was displaced by efficient use or captured by simple passive and active solar heating, and about 90 per cent of the household electricity bill has been saved, reducing its cost to £3 per month. We could still save more if we wanted to.

You could think of the building as a 1.3 barrel a day oil well because it produces about £12 worth of saved energy per day. The cost of the techniques that achieved all the savings actually paid for itself in the first ten months. Today we can do a lot better. For example, the windows are now twice as good but cost less.

BENEFICIAL EFFECTS

The most interesting thing about the building is not the technologies or even their integration. The point is that you feel better in this building. We put our board of directors round the dining-room table every autumn and they stay alert and cheerful all day. If we put the same people in an ordinary office they become sleepy and irritable in half an hour. The natural light, good air quality, lack of mechanical noise, the sound of the waterfall, the combination of low air temperature with high radiant temperature and high humidity, and perhaps other things which we don't even know about, create a much healthier environment. You feel better and you can do more and better quality work in such a building.

Cost-saving principles
One key cost-saving principle used in green architecture is to try to get multiple benefits from single expenditures. This goes beyond just

saving energy and capital costs. For example, superwindows, such as those already mentioned, save energy in three ways: cooling, heating and delivering the heat and coolness to the space. They produce better radiant comfort by bouncing your body heat back at you in the winter and excluding unwanted heat in the summer, so if you're sitting next to the window on the sunny side you don't feel as if you want to be turned on a spit and basted occasionally. Therefore you don't need to blow so much hot or cold air at yourself to maintain comfort. That saves more heating, cooling and fan energy so you can eliminate or at least downsize the heating, ventilating, and air-conditioning equipment.

There are indirect construction-cost benefits that save even more money than eliminating that equipment. For example, you can go from big rectangular ducts to small round ducts. These cost about 70 per cent less, and they save even more on labour. They also mean that if you have a dropped ceiling to hide the ducts you can make that plenum smaller – or better still, eliminate it in favour of underfloor displacement ventilation – and get in, for example, six storeys where the regulation height allows five, so the economics improve. The smaller ducts, smaller wiring closets and smaller mechanical rooms mean you can get a 5 or 6 per cent increase in space efficiency. Collectively these are very valuable savings.

In climates as severe as Stockholm in Sweden or Calgary in Canada you can also use the radiant comfort of superwindows to eliminate perimeter-zone heating – the little radiators under the windows. This saves capital cost. It saves 5 per cent or so of the floor space in perimeter offices and you can move things round without running into the radiators. That by itself pays for the extra cost of the windows. You also have better control of ultra-violet, decreasing fading of finishes and furnishings. The heavy-gas fill which the windows contain is very good at stopping noise, so you can use difficult sites; this has additional cost advantages in urban settings. There is no condensation on the inner side of the glass, which stays warm and dry, so the sash doesn't rot. It's much easier to admit and control natural light, which saves lighting energy and capacity. You start to see from this sort of list that there's a set of knock-on effects which collectively mean that if you want an inexpensive building – to construct as well as to operate – the key is often to use expensive windows.

Improving office buildings

Big savings are often cheaper than small savings in big and small buildings, hot and cold climates, new and retrofit buildings, lighting and hot-water systems, computer design, even car design. You can not only get multiple benefits from single expenditures, but you can also piggy-back on a retrofit that was going to be done anyway, for some other reason.

For example, on a 200,000 square-foot (about 18,590 square-metre) curtain-wall office building in Chicago we found we could replace old glazing that let in only 9 per cent of light by superwindows that let in nearly six times as much light, yet insulated and blocked sound about four times better. We could bounce daylight all the way in, flooding the whole floor plate with very uniform, glare-free, natural light. We could use very efficient lighting systems, which dim according to how much daylight is present, and very efficient office equipment, thereby decreasing the internal heat gain – other than from people – by 85 per cent.

Because Chicago gets very hot and humid in the summer, the building had 750 tons of 20-year-old cooling equipment in need of renovation. Normally you would just replace it with the same thing, getting rid of the CFCs (chlorofluoro-carbons) making it a little less efficient. You would end up paying almost £380,000 just to renew the moving bits and change the refrigerant. Instead you could make the system four times as efficient and about four times smaller and save almost £127,000. You save more money making the system smaller than you pay extra to make it more efficient. The saved money then pays for the lighting and daylighting retrofit and the superwindows. We would then expect to save three quarters of the energy, over £7 per square metre a year, with a simple payback between minus five and plus nine months – that is, it cost essentially the same as the routine 20-year renovation. The building would also be much nicer. It would be much easier to recruit and retain tenants because it would be such a pleasant space, quite apart from costing less.

But to do this requires highly integrated design rather than throwing one's own bit of the design over the transom to the next specialist. It requires, in other words, team play not a relay race. It requires that you optimize the whole building as a system. What normally happens is that a value engineer comes along and tells the client that the windows are too dear and he can supply cheaper ones – but then you need more cooling and more fan capacity. It's like squeezing a balloon; it pops out somewhere else. By optimizing each component separately, it's quite easy to pessimize the system. With an integrated green design, we end up optimizing the whole building as a system and, preferably, rewarding the designers for what they save, not for what they spend.

The improvements to the Chicago building never went ahead. The property was controlled by a letting agent who was incentivized on deals per month. They didn't want to delay the commissions a few months while doing a retrofit, so they didn't retrofit. They were then unable to let the building – nobody wanted to be in such an expensive and unpleasant space – so it had to be sold off at a reduced price. This illustrates that there are complex institutional barriers involved.

There are, however, good incentives to overcome those market failures. There are over 100,000 big all-glass-and-no-windows offices in the United States that are more than 20 years old. There are quite a few around London. When those have been improved there will be lots more ready for improvement.

The White House
The White House is a huge complex incorporating, among other things, a private residence, a large office building, a military base, a

botanical garden, a National Park, and an art museum. We had the honour of being involved in greening it. The Old Executive Office Building had a brilliantly designed Victorian passive cooling system, the forebear of the one in the Queen's Building at De Montfort University (see next page). Over the years it became disused and blocked up but then the old records about it were discovered. We hope to restore the system and combine it with superwindows and efficient lights, making the whole building a lot better than it was before. I would love to see the same thing done at 10 Downing Street.

Making piping more efficient
The types of savings we can make are as applicable to industry as to buildings. In a typical pumping system it takes nine units of fuel to deliver one unit of flow, so if you save one unit of flow or friction in a pipe you will save nine units of fuel and pollution at the power plant. You also save several units of size and therefore reduce the capital cost of the pump and other parts of the system. It's amazing what happens when engineers start to see how whole-system optimization works. They wonder why they ever did it differently.

One simple improvement available in all buildings is to lay out the pipes before the equipment. It is normally done the other way round, which means that the pipes have to go through all sorts of curlicues. As soon as you start giving the pipe a straight shot and putting the equipment at the ends, the whole system works better and costs less. This plus whole-system optimization — so fat, short, straight pipes were used instead of skinny, long, crooked pipes — recently saved 92 per cent of the pumping power in a standard industrial pumping loop, whilst reducing capital cost and improving performance.

Cost-effective lighting and cooling systems
Whole-system design, like a good cooking recipe, combines the right ingredients in the right mannner, sequence, and proportions.

In a lighting system, for example, you don't just put in more efficient lights and ballasts and better fixture optics, which will save 70 to 90 per cent of the energy. If you really want to do it right, you first adapt the space to help light bounce round better, to put the light up on the ceiling as God intended and then move it on into the next space, to adjust the lights according to the actual conditions and what that person's eyes want at that time. Most of all, you improve the quality of light, preferably by bouncing it off the ceiling because then, with less glare off the paper, you can see as well with about a fifth as much light.

Similarly, if you wanted to help people feel cool in a hot climate, you would go through approximately five or even seven steps, first expanding the range of conditions in which people feel comfortable. For example, if you sit on a net or mesh ventilative chair you'll be about four Centigrade degrees cooler than if you sit on an insulating upholstered chair. You can buy another seven Centigrade degrees by getting vertical air movement from a ceiling fan, and even more with improved radiant comfort. You can reduce the cooling load in the building, as we intended for the Chicago office, by a factor of typically three or four, sometimes five, by making the windows, other shell elements and equipment in the building very efficient. You can also use alternative cooling systems – ventilative, radiative, ground-coupling, absorption, desiccant or evaporative. If all these things are carried out in an integrated way, in the right order, they will suffice anywhere in the world. Of course, refrigerative cooling can also be made severalfold more efficient, but doing the right things in the right order can make it unnecessary.

The Queen's Building, De Montfort University, Leicester
This British building by Alan Short and his colleagues is a large engineering building which has been much criticized in the architectural community because not only does it have some lovely features of daylighting and very interesting complex spaces using a

difficult site well, but it is also made of brick – partly because there were a lot of highly-skilled, out-of-work bricklayers in Leicester. The building does not need any cooling or air-handling systems because of a complex series of channels permitting air, entering through louvres, to pass through and be drawn up by a draught created by draught towers. The air going through little channels creates air movement and coolness without needing fans.

This works very well even though there are some quite severe loads. There is very little heat gain inside from lighting because of the natural light, but the machine-shops have up to 9 watts a square foot of heat gain and yet the building is still nicely cooled passively.

ING Bank Building, Amsterdam
The ING Bank (formerly NMB), which bought Barings, asked architects to come up with an organic building that would integrate art, natural material, sunlight, green plants, quiet and water, but which would not cost more than a conventional building. The design team was unusually integrative. As well as architects, engineers and contractors, it included landscapers, artists and people who would use and operate the building. It took longer and cost more to design but less to build. The building is largely passively heated, cooled and ventilated. It uses one fifth the energy of a contemporary bank building nearby. Every room has natural air and natural light, and it is very quiet. Bits of coloured metal on the walls tint the light as it comes down so that it changes into all sorts of different colours during the day as the sun angle moves and the body's appetite for light changes.

This is now the best-known building in the Netherlands, apart from the Parliament. The bank rose from fourth to second in size in the country, then bought Barings. There has been a 15 per cent gain in labour productivity. People also work longer hours because they don't want to leave such a nice place. They have started running all sorts of social and community functions in it.

This project brings home the point about the bottom line again.

If you look at the costs of operating a typical office building you find that you pay about a hundred times as much for the people who work in the building as for the energy to run it. This means that if you had a 1 per cent gain in labour productivity through helping people to see what they're doing, feeling more comfortable and hearing themselves think, that would have the same bottom-line effect as eliminating the entire energy bill. In eight buildings that we have documented – and others that we are in the process of documenting – we are finding not a 1 per cent but a 6 to 16 per cent gain in labour productivity.[3]

Green ideals
Green design goes far beyond balancing heat gains and losses and the natural flows of light and air. You could say it extends infinitely outward in the six directions, as well as over time. It has much broader ambitions than saving energy. It seeks to heal natural and human communities, to do no harm, to regenerate and restore, to create an abundance of energy and water, food and health, tranquillity and beauty, to design with nature. It is about doing what a place requires.

Green design is also very mindful of where materials come from and where they go. It doesn't take the rain forests away from the orang-utan to make plywood which is thrown away after one use. It doesn't destroy anything that it can't recreate. Rather, it creates more diverse and abundant life than it borrows. It doesn't take as much in quantity or in quality as it gives back. It doesn't steal from our children but leaves them a greener and richer and more peaceful world. And it uses materials that not only regenerate themselves but also protect the health and uplift the spirit of the people who use them.

The principles of green design treat water not as cubic metres of flow but as habitat. It uses water to enhance life, to create even more diverse and beautiful conditions in which life can thrive. It makes water leaving the building and the site cleaner than the water arriving. It helps water flow where it has always wanted to flow, through the capillaries and arteries of the earth, rather than diverting it through sewer-like concrete pipes.

The Village Homes Project, California
Near Sacramento, California, there is a housing development that puts these principles into practice. Developers Mike and Judy Corbett had the idea that the site plan should involve interlocking networks of small roads coming in from one side and foot- and bike-paths coming in from the other side, with the houses in between and facing the pathways. The houses themselves are in different styles and were built by many different builders. Cars are discreetly kept round the back in rather narrow streets, although you don't actually need to drive much since you can walk or bike to most of the places that you need to get to. Community facilities include the day-care centre and extensive recreational facilities, so you can really spend most of your life in the village.

There are lots of gardens; residents do their own organic farming and gardening. The landscaping, paid for by the civil works avoided by using drainage swales, became so extensive that if you want breakfast you just go out and see what's ripe. The residents cover most of the costs of the home-owners' association by the sale of the organic almond harvest; they also make money from selling fruits and vegetables in the market. This all pays for the parks. The residents end up with an extraordinary quality of life.

This project started off being so weird that the agents wouldn't show it. Now it's the most desirable place in town and houses sell in less than a third of the normal time at almost a £7 premium per square foot. Most sell by word of mouth before they're even listed.

There are many other aspects of green design that go still further, that focus on people getting access to the places they want to enjoy, including old and young people, poor or infirm people. It integrates buildings with purposes and people. It favours walking and bicycling over cars and trains, and makes sure that you can get to public transport conveniently if you want to. It reduces isolation and fosters neighbourliness. It protects street life, the public realm, the neighbourhood and the community. It designs communities round people, not round cars. In the Village Homes community the crime rate is approximately one tenth that of neighbouring, conventionally-designed areas, because there are more eyes on the street; there is more defensible space; and there is a vibrant street life.

Green buildings' connections to the community run as deep as any tap root, and the links are not only physical but economic, communitarian and spiritual.

Incentivizing green design

To encourage more understanding and use of green architectural principles, the current perverse incentives must be changed. We may need a way to share cost savings between the landlord and tenants so they all have an incentive to adopt green design. Designers' compensation is traditionally based on what they spend. That is, it's traditionally calculated from a base of a percentage of the cost of the building or the cost of the equipment specified. Then it's negotiated downwards from there to a level that doesn't support real design any more. If instead, or in addition, the design team were given three years' worth of energy savings, that would be enough to double or even treble the design fee – and would certainly get the designers' attention. For the first time they would be rewarded for doing a better job. There are serious discussions in progress with the American, German and Swiss architectural professional associations on how to arrange this, and I hope the same discussion can be started by UK architects and engineers. Then we can move on to sort out the perverse incentives that influence all the other parties in the building process so that we can get reintegrated design, real optimization and rational incentives all round.

References

1   Rocky Mountain Institute (1997), RMI Publication D97-11, New York: John Wiley.

2   Rocky Mountain Institute (1997), RMI Publication D97-12, Snowmass, Colorado, USA, www.rmi.org.

3   Romm, J.J. and Browning, W.D. (1994), *Greening the Building and the Bottom Line: Increasing Productivity through Energy-Efficient Design*, RMI Publication D94-27, Snowmass, Colorado 81654, USA: Rocky Mountain Institute, www.rmi.org.

THE CONTRIBUTION OF ARCHITECTURE TO SUSTAINABLE DEVELOPMENT

*Department of Environmental Social Sciences, Keele University;
Programme Director, Forum for the Future*

A s an environmental economist I have, I hope, gained some understanding of what sustainable development might be, and I believe that the broad principles of architecture can contribute to the process of sustainable development.

Sustainable development is becoming the organizing framework for thinking about the environment. There has been an enormous amount written about it, much of it rather confusing, and in the academic literature and popular utterances on the subject you often find people throwing in the word 'sustainable' as an alternative perhaps to the word 'nice' or 'desirable'. That seems to me to be a very undesirable state of affairs. Some, indeed, believe that 'sustainable development' has been so corrupted by this kind of verbal abuse that the term has become almost meaningless, but I don't agree with that perspective.

Defining sustainable development
One can get a long way simply by focusing on the normal common-sense meanings of the words. Development is something that economists in particular but others, too, have thought about for a very long time. Its normal meaning is something like 'the achievement of potential and the improvement of the quality of

life'. When economists think about the quality of life they have tended perhaps too much to think in terms of increasing income per head, and indeed quite a lot of the development literature equates development with growth of Gross National Product. That is an error in theoretical terms and I'm pleased to say that increasingly, through such publications as *The Human Development Report* of the United Nations Development Programme[1], it is becoming more widely perceived as an error.

There are clearly a multitude of factors that contribute to development, to the quality of our lives. Not only is there income but there is income distribution. Then there is employment, working conditions and the obverse of employment – leisure. Then of course there is the environment, and some have added security. The political problem, of course, is what weights to attach to those different factors, what kinds of trade-offs to allow between those various contributions to development.

The second word of our composite concept is 'sustainable', which literally means 'it can go on for a long time'. One of the conclusions which is now not quite absolute but certainly commonplace among reputable thinkers is that whatever process of development we may have had over the last 50 years, it has not been sustainable. That is to say, it cannot go on.

Support for sustainable development

I will not explore here all the evidence for unsustainability that has caused people to come to that kind of conclusion, but a range of organizations have studied the available evidence in some detail, and the one thing they appear to be agreed about is that the development process that we know, that we have known perhaps since the Industrial Revolution, is not sustainable. These organizations include the World Business Council for Sustainable Development, the World Resources Institute (one of the best-known Washington think-tanks on the environment), the European Fifth Action Programme on the Environment, the

World Watch Institute, the UK Royal Society and US National Academy of Sciences.

It is particularly significant that the UK Royal Society and the US National Academy of Sciences are included in this list. Very often people say that the kinds of utterances made by environmentalists are extreme and hysterical, so I was intrigued that at the time of the Rio Earth Summit in 1992, these two organizations, two of the foremost scientific institutions in the world, produced their first-ever joint communiqué. It arrived at the conclusion that not only was our development process unsustainable but that 'the future of our planet is in the balance'[2]. That seems a fairly strong kind of statement to make, but it was probably made on the basis of some fairly rigorous scientific thought.

It was that kind of perception that caused the world's politicians and leaders in Rio, at the then largest-ever gathering of heads of state and heads of government, to embrace wholeheartedly the concept of sustainable development. By itself this said little more than, 'Well, if this process of development is unsustainable we must have one which is sustainable.' I suspect many of them thought that once they went home that would be the end of it.

The sustainability experiment
In fact, what we have embarked on in seeking to find a process of sustainable development is an extraordinary experiment, because it is something of which we have absolutely no experience. The defining characteristic of the industrial economic process since the Industrial Revolution has probably been the conversion of natural capital, of environmental resources of all kinds, into both manufactured capital – machines, factories, roads, infrastructure and so on – and human capital, such as knowledge and education. Still today many countries that are well endowed with natural resources, but not perhaps as well endowed as they would like with the other forms of capital, perceive that the way in which they can develop is to liquidate their

natural resources as fast as they can and to convert, for example, forests into car factories.

It is precisely that process which has lain at the heart of the development that we have known, which people like the UK Royal Society and the US National Academy of Sciences have said is unsustainable. This is not a moral judgement, although you can draw moral conclusions from it. It is a positive statement in the scientific sense, meaning simply that it cannot go on. Why? Obviously, we live in a planet which is finite physically and therefore to continue to convert a finite quantity of physical resources into other kinds of capital is not a process that can continue indefinitely.

All sorts of other questions are thrown up by this – fascinating questions, given that we have no real firsthand knowledge of what a sustainable development process would be like. What kind of development process would it be that didn't systematically convert natural capital into other kinds of capital? Is such a development process compatible with continuing indefinite economic growth throughout society and the global community at large? Is it compatible with what we have come to call our society, a 'consumer' society? Is that a model for a sustainable development process? Most radical of all perhaps, especially in these days when socialism has been collapsing with great speed round the world, is a sustainable development process compatible with capitalism?

We do not yet know the answers to these questions because we have not yet achieved a sustainable development process. The only way we can find out the answers is to decide what some of the objectives of environmental sustainability might be and then see what we need to do to pursue those objectives.

Conditions for sustainable development
Here is my list of six conditions that I believe would need to be satisfied for a development process to be called sustainable. Sustainability:

- should not destabilize the climate;
- should not be allowed to destroy the ozone layer;
- should ensure that the basic structure of the biosphere, namely its biodiversity, is conserved;
- should ensure that renewable resources are renewed and that non-renewable resources are not depleted faster than the development of substitutes that could enable the functions of the resources to continue indefinitely;
- should ensure that the emissions from our industry and from our lifestyles into the environment − air, soil and water − are not so great that the natural systems of the environment cannot absorb and neutralize them over time;
- should ensure that the risks of life-damaging events of a potentially catastrophic nature should not be taken.

Those are fairly tough conditions. To take the first one, the Intergovernmental Panel on Climate Change in its first report for the Rio summit concluded that in order to stabilize the climate we would need to cut carbon dioxide emissions globally by a minimum of 60 per cent from 1990 levels. Yet there are many countries that consume far fewer fossil fuels than we do and that are determined to increase their consumption of fossil fuels in order to develop. Therefore the implications for a society like ours of that kind of sustainability condition are clearly fairly serious.

Over the last fifteen or twenty years we have discovered an enormous amount about many things relating to sustainability. We know by and large which sectors are the problem. They were spelt out in the European Commission's Fifth Action Programme on the Environment of 1992, to which our country, along with all the other European Union countries, is a signatory: energy, transport, agriculture, tourism, some industrial process and waste management − no great surprises there.

We also know, at least in terms of the first few steps, what needs to be done in order to move towards more sustainable patterns of development. Some of our societies, including the UK, have even taken the first tentative steps in those directions. But for the general consensus – among scientists – one need only look at one sector, transport. The report of the Royal Commission on Environmental Pollution in 1994[3] covered the transport sector and made it perfectly clear that we are moving much too slowly.

Obstacles to progress

Why are we moving so slowly towards a process of sustainable development when it appears that there's very broad consensus about the problems and some of the necessary solutions? There are basically three reasons, and they are very understandable.

On the producer side many companies have evolved patterns of production which depend on the unsustainable use of resources. They perceive moves to sustainability as a threat to their profitability and some of them are determined to stop such moves altogether or slow them down. The net result is that we move very slowly.

Then there are institutional difficulties. The UK Conservative Government's White Paper on the environment in 1990 identified very clearly that the problems of actually getting environmental issues integrated across Whitehall are enormous. While some of the measures in the paper might have helped, nobody imagines that it's a problem that has been fully solved. Similarly, in firms we find that the environment is not a traditional core business concern, and putting the environment into firms' agendas is a slow and sometimes painful process.

Given that both Government and firms have nevertheless made enormous strides in many areas in the last five to ten years trying to internalize this agenda, the major problem seems to be that of consumers. We must frankly acknowledge that many people get a lot of pleasure from doing things which have a harmful effect on the environment and they are unwilling not to do those things or they don't perceive they have any alternative but to do those things. I think the fascinating debate that we are currently having at a social level about transport, motor cars and related issues is a good example of that.

So we arrive at the situation whereby sustainable development is not only technically feasible, it's also economically achievable. Fascinating work has been done that shows that the net cost of moving towards sustainable development need not be very great. There will be winners and losers, but for society as a whole the net cost, in the early stages at least, need not be very great. We tend to muddle along, hoping that the scientists are wrong, hoping that by the time the balloon goes up we at least will be dead or hoping that some technical fix will show up. We want to be sustainable, but not yet, because being unsustainable can still be a lot of fun. The risk is that we will set in train irreversible processes which at worst will make this planet much less inhabitable than it currently is for our species. We must remember that at the moment it is a planet that will have to support at least twice as many people as it currently does support.

The contribution of architecture
What is it that architects might do to address this? My perception is that they can do a lot. Buildings consume something like 50 per cent of the fossil fuels that are used in the UK. They have an enormous impact on the countryside, on transport patterns, on aesthetics and on a sense of community. The last two elements are very important components of development and it may well be that we will have to make trade-offs in rebuilding community and developing a finer aesthetic sense of our environments to compensate for, perhaps, reduced car use. We may need to focus on other aspects of the human experience which can give us satisfaction, which can be part of a development but which do not involve converting natural resources to wastes.

Obviously, an enormous part of this process of tackling buildings is to do with upgrading existing buildings, given that they are probably the most long-lived products which we create. I sense, from having talked to a few, that architects don't regard that as a terribly glamorous task, although one can see some programmes of refurbishment which have been done in line with sustainable-development thinking and which move towards the sustainability conditions that I have outlined. These projects have been imaginative, aesthetically pleasing, exciting and have substantially reduced the environmental impact of the buildings concerned.

But the fact that we only replace or add to a very small percentage of our housing stock each year does not seem to me to diminish greatly the role of new build in sustainable development, for several reasons. First, sustainable development is a multi-decade task. It is not something that we are going to achieve in one generation, so even less than one per cent per year, over thirty or forty years, can translate into something very substantial. More than that, I think buildings have a huge symbolic importance. They are very visible. Buildings that were obviously constructed to make efficient use of resources, and which advertise that fact, seem to me to be an important living advertisement for many of the changes which we will need to take.

Principles of sustainable architecture
Many architects have recognized these points. This was clear from the 1993 Declaration of Interdependence for a Sustainable Future[4] which was the theme of the 1993 World Congress of Architects in Chicago, organized by the American Institute of Architects and the International Union of Architects. Those who attended identified some of the principles which they thought should be at the heart of an architecture for sustainable development. They felt that:

- sustainability should be at the core of architectural practice and of professional responsibilities;
- there should be continual improvement in sustainable design;
- architects have a duty to educate their profession and their peer colleagues about sustainable development;

- they should lobby Government to increase environmental standards so that it becomes easier to gain the experience in sustainable design which is needed;
- the concept of sustainable design should stretch right the way through the lifecycle of products used to construct the buildings up to their disposal.

One of the advisers to that congress put his wishlist like this[4]:

- building materials should have overall a benign environmental impact;
- buildings should be minimal consumers of energy and other resources throughout their lifecycle;
- buildings should have healthy and pleasing internal environments;
- buildings should foster community;
- buildings should be so arranged that there are accessible green spaces in urban areas;
- buildings should enable a kind of transport infrastructure to be developed round them such that there is easy access to the daily necessities of life with only the optional use of the private motor car.

Affordability
In the UK a pioneering group called the Designers' Collaborative has come up with its wishlist for architecture for the twenty-first century entailing ecological sensitivity, the avoidance of pollution, maximum energy efficiency, including the embodied energy in buildings, an appropriate level of building autonomy, a contribution to community life and, most importantly from my point of view, financial affordability.

This issue of affordability is key, because no wishlist in the world is any good in a market-driven economy if there are cheaper alternatives which are perceived by the client to do the job just as well. Economists call this phenomenon 'externalities'. We perceive that one of the problems that has contributed to a lot of environmental destruction is that it's very easy for people to generate costs and then pass them on to the environment rather than internalizing them themselves in their own cost structures. If it remains cheap to waste energy, to pollute land, water and air and generally behave with low environmental responsibility, and if raising this level of responsibility requires investment, then architects will find it no less difficult than other businesses and professionals to argue for or absorb costs which others are externalizing on to society at large.

This is one of the defining issues of our time. We have grown up, our institutions have developed, our businesses have evolved and our laws and investments have been made with a certain perception about the availability of environmental goods. Very often the perception has been that those goods will be free, whether we are talking about air and emissions to air, water and emissions to water or, in many countries, trees and timber. These have just been things that people have assumed will be there for the asking and for the taking. It's now quite apparent that they are not free; even the atmosphere is not free. Yet trying to ensure that the people who use the atmosphere pay for that use, when everything we do has been posited on the assumption that it is free, is an extremely difficult business.

Government action

This problem is one that only Government can resolve. There are instruments which it can, in theory at least, readily use to accomplish this task, such as the tax system. An enormous amount of work has now been carried out on what might happen to the economy if a government decided that it was systematically going to shift a large part of the burden of taxation from labour and the profits of capital on to the use of natural resources. The good news is that it's clearly very possible to do this without major economic disruption. There are some conditions which one would need to apply in order to bring about this happy result. One is that we don't try to do it too fast. Another is that we allow companies that have made substantial investments in natural-resource-intensive sectors to derive some profits from those investments while government sends the clearest possible signals to future investors that new investments must be made on the basis that environmental goods will have to be paid for at an escalating rate. Clearly, if government is getting its taxes from the taxes on environmental goods, it can reduce taxes elsewhere. This is a shift of burden rather than its overall increase or decrease.

It is disappointing that in the present climate of discussion about taxation (which seems to be that the only politically safe thing to say about tax is that you will minimize it), this kind of issue cannot be debated in a manner commensurate with its importance. It is literally inconceivable in a market economy that we will start to take care of the environment unless it figures in prices. Prices are what drive resource allocation in a market, and if we continue to price environmental resources either for free or for much less than their social costs we can continue to expect that they will be abused and overused with much attendant human and environmental disruption.

Combining financial and environmental benefits
Some architects believe that green architecture is concerned with buildings that use the earth's resources lightly and that are expressive of a way of living that thinks in terms of partnership with nature. You could define like that any of the human activities which we need to change, for example transport. It's clear that a minority of architects have embraced such a concept with enthusiasm and have striven to absorb the extra costs which this enthusiasm sometimes leads to. But the majority won't, and they probably can't while it is cheaper and more profitable and legal to destroy the environment.

My very economistic conclusion is that we won't be serious about sustainable development, and we can't be serious about sustainable development, in a market economy like ours until it is financially rational as well as environmentally beneficial and morally right. I look forward to the day when sustainable architecture or green architecture can take its place in that kind of framework.

References
1   UNDP (United Nations Development Report) annual *Human Development Report*, Oxford/New York: Oxford University Press.
2   Royal Society and National Academy of Sciences (1992), *Population Growth, Resource Consumption and a Sustainable World*, London: Royal Society and New York: National Academy of Sciences.
3   Royal Commission on Environmental Pollution (1994), *Transport and the Environment*, 18th Report, London: HMSO.
4   Gilman, R. (1993), 'It's Time to Rebuild!', *In Context*, No. 35, June, Bainbridge Island, Washington: Context Institute.

SHOULD GREEN ARCHITECTURE BE SOMETHING DIFFERENT?

ALEXANDROS N. TOMBAZIS

Architect, A. N. Tombazis & Associates

We have thought of so many words for the subject of green architecture – such as solar or environmentally friendly architecture or bioclimatic design, but do they really mean something different after all? In 30 years of work as an architect I have found that one of the most fascinating things in architecture is its hidden inner beauty, the things one can't see, the things that one should be able to feel. It is this beauty that I shall discuss in the context of environmentally friendly design.

Common misconceptions
There are two main misconceptions. The first one is that green, solar or bioclimatic architecture has to look different, but it does not. Green architecture is not, thank goodness, a style. Despite all the 'isms' that have come and gone, and all that are still around, green architecture is something different, something more profound, and something that is here to stay.

The second misconception is that solar architecture cannot work in cloudy conditions, which is also wrong. It all depends on what we make of the buildings, how we conceive them, how we design them, and how they function. Every building on this planet is solar in some way, but there are bad ones and better ones. So whether it's cloudy or sunny, there are things to think about and things to take care about, though different places need different solutions.

Holistic principles

One of the beauties of architecture is that it is so complex. It has to be built as a set of conditions, and it has to be comprehensive in its approach. The green part of architecture is only a small part of the whole comprehensive picture. We should never think that we are at the beginning or the end of the picture. We are only part of it and part of the whole process of architectural design. Bioclimatic design is a design of balances. Everything is happening at the same time. What is important is the end result of the combination of all the balances. If one issue is overemphasized, you lose the total picture.

Barriers to green architecture

Why is there so much architecture that still ignores these facts? Why are there so many architects who are indifferent to or ignorant of these issues?

One answer is the option of the easy way out. The day that the architect, the general public or any user could turn a switch to change night into day or make the most humid, horrible, hot conditions cool and soothing was the beginning of architectural wrongdoings. It was too easy. We could just do whatever we wanted. In the past one had to be a bit more clever – traditional, vernacular architecture did not have the means to do what we can do today. This is what is really one of the core problems today: it's just too easy to do whatever we want.

Many students don't learn the basics of how the earth moves round the sun. On far too many architectural drawings we are not even shown where the north is, which gives an indication of the values given by teaching. This is a failure that can, of course, be remedied during working life, but it is very important to start early. Thank goodness there are more and more colleges throughout the world that are addressing these issues properly.

Another barrier to green design is that we are too fond, as architects, of inventing non-existent problems. We want to have a preconceived idea of what we want to achieve and then we invent our own set of problems so we can respond to these non-existent design parameters. This is another failure. I think the way to look at this is as follows. There are so many problems that are already there to respond to, because one cannot design in a vacuum, that we don't have to invent anything. We just have to have our eyes open to be able to respond in the right way.

There is also a fear of constraints. All architects are afraid of constraints and say they are given too much to think about, but the opposite is true. As I said, you cannot design in a vacuum. Constraints are something which you have to respond to. Architects do not need to feel free as a bird flying up in the sky and constraints do not drag you down. We tend to be fearful that balanced solutions will be mediocre – if there isn't that extra something to it, then it won't be good enough – but that also is wrong, because that extra something doesn't have to be only visual.

Architects are sometimes wary of technical issues. They feel that technical issues relating to green design are above their head or they cannot be bothered with them. It is the way in which such issues are presented that is to blame and, again, the way that architects are educated.

Another problem is the ego of the architect. We think we are the centre of the world, and that prevents us from thinking rationally and communicating properly. But architecture is all about communicating, and if we can't communicate with the rest of the design team, and society in general, we shouldn't be practising architecture.

The big issue is what is architecture all about? Is it an art, a technique or what? The problem is that we think of architecture – the general public and architects too – as mostly visual. We look with our eyes and we think no further – we feel no further. We think we're looking, we think we're seeing, we think we're understanding, but it's a blind man's perception of architecture if you can go no further than just a picture in a glossy magazine and can't understand what's happening inside. Architecture is much more than pure art.

Key characteristics of bioclimatic design
What are the most important ingredients of bioclimatic design? The first is context. Architecture has to be designed within context. It is context that ties architecture to everything around it, whether natural landscape, man-made landscape or whatever. The first thing which should happen in all architecture, and certainly in bioclimatic or environmentally friendly architecture, is to think of it within its context. Every case is a unique case.

Another important principle of bioclimatic design is that less is beautiful. 'Less' does not mean that there isn't enough, but that there is a minimum need, a minimum quantity for every situation, and that is what bioclimatic design is all about. Minimum quantity does not necessarily mean quantity itself. It is the minimum things you have to do, the minimum performance, the minimum of everything, but that which is adequate, so it does not mean less in the sense of too little. This in itself is beautiful. It is also to do with simplicity.

Another key principle of bioclimatic design is thinking of buildings as living organisms. Every building is just as alive as all of us. It perspires, it breathes, it feels cold, it feels hot, it should shade itself – it should do all these things when necessary. What it doesn't have is a voice to shout back and say how stupid we have been in condemning it to one place when it doesn't have a pair of legs to run away. Metaphorically the building should be able to put on a pullover when it needs to; it should be able to take off clothes when it needs to.

Process versus product
Another point that we should be considering and dealing with is

the different ways of approaching the design process. We should be caring less about the end product and more about the process. The end product will be the result of understanding the principles, and the principles of bioclimatic design are the principles which have been around for many, many years. There is nothing new. What is different is the scientific analysis, the research, the measurements, the monitoring, all of the understanding procedures. So this kind of design is not some new kind of 'fix'; it is something which is as old as mankind, but we have the means today, and the reasoning, to look at it and to understand the principles. We should be learning from but not imitating the past. The more we learn about the past, the less we can imitate it. It means that we are understanding what has gone on and that we learn from the principles and from the procedure, but not by imitating.

Thinking beneath the surface

Architects should be inventive and not take things for granted. We should not think of windows and building materials just in a pictorial way, deciding whether they are aesthetically acceptable or not. We should get under their skin, dispute everything and think about such things in a rational way. For example, we should think of the skin of a building as like the skin of a plant, animal or human being, and consider how important and intricate it is, how many different things are happening in it. Then we can try to create buildings in the same way. The building's skin could be made up of layers; it could have different objectives. It is not just a case of whether it has to be marble, granite or glass. There can be many ways of using these same materials in a more imaginative and creative way.

Thinking ahead

It is important for architects to foresee the future. Most of the services and mechanical equipment in buildings today are there because of the stupid mistakes that we have made, and engineers spend their time sorting them out. Most of what has been installed need not have been put there in the first place. We should practise preventive medicine instead of just curing when it's too late. That's how we should approach bioclimatic design and architecture in general.

Hidden dimensions

Architectural design typically allows for some of the five senses, but not all of them. When we design we tend to think with our eyes. We forget about touch and sound, for example. We design buildings as if there is nothing in them, but there is air everywhere, and air behaves according to the laws of physics. It never keeps quiet and it moves up when it's warm. This generates a whole lot of practical issues when designing architecture. If we think of air, we won't think of a building with our eyes in the way that we did before.

We also tend to ignore time. Buildings respond to time, or they should. They are not the same in the morning as in the evening or the same in spring as in winter. Time relates to climate, to the whole universe. If we think of the building as a living organism, we should think of it as responding, evolving and reacting to time.

Architecture could not exist without light, but we too often rely on artificial rather than natural light. It is useful for the architect to 'change hats' during the design process and reconsider everything in terms of how it responds to light, time, air and all the other issues that tend to be forgotten. If you do this in a more analytical way, then bring the issues together, it results in a much more profound and climatically and environmentally responsive design.

In our office in Athens, built in 1995, we are consuming about 40 or 45 kilowatt hours per square metre for everything, when usually offices in Greece consume about 400 or 500, depending on whether they are air-conditioned or not. But that is not the most important factor. It is a much more agreeable and much more natural space in which to work, as well as being an office that is helping the planet.

Green architecture is about the hidden dimensions of architecture and design. It is about the maze of intricate balances, the unending mesh of profound and important issues that − apart from being of vital importance to mankind − are in themselves beautiful and wonderful constraints and starting blocks for creative design.

During the design process we must be sure to consider:

- scale;
- position, context and orientation;
- shape, compactness or openness;
- response to climate and time;
- treatment of the skin of the building as a harvester of or protector from the sun, wind and water;
- mass of the building as a storer and redistributor of energy;
- overall energy consumption and production of pollution;
- light;
- air quality;
- materials used and their embodied energy, appropriateness and production of waste;
- lifecycle analysis of the whole construction.

INFORMATION ON RSA PROGRAMMES

The RSA's programmes focus primarily on business and industry, design and technology, education, the arts and the environment. Projects, which range from campaigns and enquiries, sometimes leading to a publication, to award schemes are largely self-funded with money coming from a variety of sources including trusts, foundations, companies and government. Some projects develop and grow to such an extent as to warrant independent status and they become 'spin-off' organizations. Examples include the RSA Examinations Board, Centre for Tomorrow's Company, Campaign for Learning and National Advisory Council for Careers and Educational Guidance (NACCEG).

Current RSA projects include:

THE ENVIRONMENT PROGRAMME

The RSA's Environment Programme is concentrating on means of motivating its 22,000 Fellows to champion sustainable practices in their workplaces and communities. The Programme is based at the RSA Centre in Bristol.

Contact: Simon Fordham, OBE, Centre Director, tel 01275 371145

THE ARTS MATTER PROGRAMME

This is a series of projects focused on arts education including:

- The Effect and Effectiveness of Arts Education in Secondary Schools

A three-year research project with the National Foundation for Educational Research documenting the range of effects and outcomes of a school-based arts education. (Publication: *The Effects and Effectiveness of Arts Education in Schools - NFER, interim report*, 1998)

- The Arts in Initial Teacher Training

  A research project documenting and assessing the current situation and future trends with respect to arts experience in the training and development of teachers. (Publication: *The Disappearing Arts?* 1998)

- Arts Audit

  A pilot project developed in Bristol to assist schools in the undertaking of an arts audit. A practical guide is available. (Publication: *Investing in the Arts*, 1998)

- Other arts publications

  Guaranteeing an entitlement to the Arts in schools, 1995; *The Arts Matter* - series of lectures, published by Gower, 1997; *Work, creativity and the arts*, 1999.

Contact: Michaela Crimmin, Head of Arts, RSA

THE ART FOR ARCHITECTURE AWARD SCHEME
This scheme encourages cross-disciplinary approaches to building and landscape projects by providing funds for artists to work as part of a design team. The emphasis is on collaboration, enabling artists to play a significant role in the initial stages of a project.

Contact: Jes Fernie, Project Manager, Art for Architecture, RSA

STUDENT DESIGN AWARDS
The Student Design Awards scheme has, over the last 75 years, become the UK's premier competition for student designers,

attracting over 3,000 entries a year for over 40 realistic and challenging briefs. The scheme encourages good practice, innovation, sustainability and responsible design solutions. (Publications: *Student Design Awards Projects* book, 1998/99; *Student Design Awards Blueprint Review*, 1997/98; *Design for Ageing Network Teaching Pack*, 1996)

Contact: Susan Hewer, Head of Design, RSA

REDEFINING SCHOOLING
This project calls for a re-engineering of the education system as a whole and is working to develop the framework of a new competence-based National Curriculum. It follows on from the recent Redefining Work project, a two-year national debate on how patterns of work are changing and the impact of these changes. (Publications: *Redefining Schooling* discussion paper, 1998; *Redefining Work* report, 1998, available from Gower)

Contact: Lesley James, Head of Education, RSA

PROJECT2001
Project2001 opens the door to qualifications for people of any age who have built up skills and competencies through experience in the voluntary sector either as volunteers or paid employees. It also offers mentors to managers in participating voluntary organizations. (Publication: *Qualified by Experience*, 1998)

Contact: Janet Fleming, Project Director, Project2001, RSA

FOCUS ON FOOD
This project is run by the RSA at Dean Clough, Halifax. It is a five-year campaign aiming to promote, develop and sustain the place of food in education.

Contact: Anita Cormac, Project Director, Focus on Food, RSA at Dean Clough (tel 01422 250250)

FORUM FOR ETHICS IN THE WORKPLACE

The Forum for Ethics in the Workplace seeks to develop high ethical standards at work. Set up in 1997 and funded by the Comino Foundation, the Forum meets regularly, bringing together a wide variety of professionals to discuss ethics in the context of work.

Contact: Susie Harries, Project Administrator, Forum for Ethics in the Workplace, RSA

OTHER CONTACTS

RSA Examinations Board (OCR)
Tel 01203 470033

The Centre for Tomorrow's Company
Mark Goyder, Director
Centre for Tomorrow's Company
Tel 0171 930 5150

Campaign for Learning
Bill Lucas, Director
Campaign for Learning
Tel 0171 930 1111

National Advisory Council for Careers and Educational Guidance (NACCEG)
Tel 01962 878340

INDEX